YOUR DAILY NUMEROLOGY

BOOKS BY SANDRA KOVACS STEIN &
CAROL ANN SCHULER:

LOVE NUMBERS: A NUMEROLOGICAL GUIDE TO COMPATIBILITY

YOUR DAILY NUMEROLOGY: A LIFETIME GUIDE FOR SUCCESS

BY SANDRA KOVACS STEIN:

INSTANT NUMEROLOGY: A MANUAL FOR THE BEGINNER

BY CAROL ANN SCHULER:

THE VIBES BOOK: A GAME OF SELF-ANALYSIS
(with Ellin Dodge Young)

YOUR DAILY NUMEROLOGY

A Lifetime Guide for Success

Sandra Kovacs Stein
and
Carol Ann Schuler

NEWCASTLE PUBLISHING CO., INC.
North Hollywood, California
1987

Copyright © 1987 by Sandra Kovacs Stein and Carol Ann Schuler
All rights reserved
ISBN 0-87877-125-5

Edited by Hank Stine and Janrae Frank
Cover/Book design by Riley K. Smith

FIRST EDITION

A NEWCASTLE BOOK

First Printing, October 1987

9 8 7 6 5 4 3 2 1

Printed in the United States of America

A time to be aggressive and a time to be passive,
A time to be together and a time to be alone,
A time to fight and a time to love,
A time to work and a time to play,
A time to cry and a time to laugh,
A time to confront and a time to withdraw,
A time to speak and a time to be silent,
A time to hurry and a time to wait.
—*Ecclesiastes* 3:1–8*

---

*As revised in: Muriel James and Dorothy Jongeward, *Born to Win* (Menlo Park, CA: Addison-Wesley, 1971), p. 3.

CONTENTS

Introduction		ix
CHAPTER I	FINDING YOUR GUIDE NUMBERS	1
CHAPTER II	THE 1 YEAR	9
CHAPTER III	THE 2 YEAR	33
CHAPTER IV	THE 3 YEAR	57
CHAPTER V	THE 4 YEAR	81
CHAPTER VI	THE 5 YEAR	105
CHAPTER VII	THE 6 YEAR	129
CHAPTER VIII	THE 7 YEAR	153
CHAPTER IX	THE 8 YEAR	177
CHAPTER X	THE 9 YEAR	201

INTRODUCTION

*Teach us to number our days
that we may apply our hearts unto wisdom.*
—Psalms 90:12

Have you ever wondered why events in your own personal life happened when they did? Why you haven't been able to make a change despite so much effort? Why you've wanted to be alone lately, when you're usually so outgoing? It's not a mystery if you know what numbers are affecting you. Whether you are aware of it or not, your numbers are constantly influencing you.

When should you forge ahead with a new project? When are you likely to meet someone new? When should you plan a party? When are you likely to move? Knowing your numbers can help you plan your course of action by courting the positive forces and steering away from the negative.

Modern numerology is not fatalistic, however. Rather, it encourages individual choice. Properly used, it can be an invaluable technique for self-awareness and self-improvement by showing you how your energies have operated in the past, how they are operating now, and how they are most likely to operate in the future—unless you decide to handle them in a different way.

Just as all of nature is regulated by rhythm and periodicity, so too are you. Nothing is permanent but change. Work alternates with rest, active with inactive periods. You cannot remain stationary, however much you try. Besides the more obvious cycles of days, weeks, seasons, and years, each one of us has a very personal cycle which is based on our date of birth. This cycle lasts for nine years, then repeats itself. Like the stages of a harvesting season, these years from 1 to 9 have their own set of influences—each one preparing for the next. In order to have a good "harvest," no step can be neglected or left out. Each year, in turn, can be broken down into months and days.

Forewarned is forearmed! Although you can't stop the tide from coming in, so to speak, you can decide whether to swim or sink or climb to safer ground. You have the choice and power to confront any situation, no matter how disagreeable it may seem at the time, and turn it to your advantage.

Using the numbers derived from your given name at birth and your birthdate, an accurate roadmap can be drawn up of your own personal vibrations and how these interrelate with those of the universe. Although many people share the same birthdate, and some people may even share the same name, the combination of a particular name and birthdate is unique. This is the reason why no two lives are ever exactly alike.

The numbers from your given name at birth describe your personality—what you are looking for in life, what you really want and need, what makes you tick. They show how you are likely to react to different situations; the first impression you make on others before they get to know you well; where your strengths, weaknesses and hidden talents lie; and what types of work you are best suited for.

On the other hand, the numbers in your birthdate describe the environments you will be exposed to at different times, the opportunities you will have and the obstacles you are likely to face.

Numerology, then, is a science of vibration that is as old as the recorded history of man. There is evidence that it was in use over ten thousand years ago in ancient Greece, Rome, Egypt and China, and it is referred to in the ancient books of wisdom such as the Indian *Vedas* and the Hebrew *Kabbalah*. There are many references to the mystical significance of numbers throughout the Old and New Testaments of the Bible (three representing the trinity, seven years of plenty followed by seven years of famine, God resting on the seventh day) as well as accounts of name changes made to alter circumstances, such as Abram to Abraham, and Simon to Peter. God promised Abraham that his wife would have a son after her name was changed from Sarai to Sarah (*Genesis* 17:15–16). Authors such as Shakespeare allude to numerical symbology as well: the "Ides of March" in *Julius Caesar* and the "divinity of odd numbers" in *The Merry Wives of Windsor*.

However, that part of numerology that we shall be dealing with in this book goes back even further, to the time when primitive man—who was dependent on the land for his survival—became aware that nature was governed by certain unbreakable laws such as the cycles and rhythms of the harvest season. He discovered that if he and his family were going to have food to eat, he could not do things haphazardly. He soon learned, for instance, that crops would not grow if the seeds were planted in the winter or fall—they had to be planted in the spring. A good harvest depended on his doing things according to a definite order. Certain steps had to be taken at very specific times.

Without the aid of modern inventions such as the telescope, people of antiquity understood the cycles of the moon and earth and the effects of the planets. Aware that life is the result of an ordered scheme of events rather than a hodge-podge of accidents, ancient scholars devised a system of numerical symbols which could represent and forecast these events, and which they could also consult for guidance. Only the priests and a special class of initiates, however, were allowed to learn the mysteries of the unseen forces. They were aware that knowledge is power and considered it dangerous for the general public to have too much of it. Ideas were usually passed on orally for fear that they might fall into the wrong hands if they were written down.

Although most of us no longer till the fields, good timing is still important, and a great deal of success depends on being in the right place at the right time. *When* we do something is often as important, if not more so, than *how* we do it.

Though there were many different numerological systems in use, the one established by the Greek philosopher Pythagoras formed the basis for modern numerology as we know it today. In the sixth century B.C., Pythagoras (also known as the father of mathematics) founded a school in which the study of music, astronomy and human behavior was combined with the theory of numbers. He taught that everything in the universe is a source of energy that vibrates at a certain rate, which in turn corresponds to a certain number. Furthermore, he determined that everything in the universe operates in predictable, progressive cycles measurable by the single digits from 1 through 9.

Over the years, the abstract symbols used to predict and measure man's character and destiny were checked and refined. Still, it remained an obscure science until only recently. At the turn of the century, an American from New Jersey, Mrs. L. Dow Balliet, made this information available to the general public by authoring several books on the subject explaining how names and numbers are connected and how they tell a story. Later, others such as Dr. Julia Seton, Florence Campbell and Juno Jordan continued to spread the word.* Today there is a proliferation of information on the subject, making it completely accessible to all who are interested.

Numerology is perhaps the simplest of all the occult sciences to work with. To set up your complete chart you need only know your name on your birth certificate and your date of birth. There are no complicated tables to consult or lengthy mathematical calculations to ponder, only the most basic addition and subtraction. (To learn how to set up a complete chart, you may wish to refer to *Instant Numerology*, by Sandra Kovacs Stein, or *The Vibes Book: A Game of Self-Analysis*, by Ellin Dodge Young and Carol Ann Schuler.) *Your Daily Numerology* deals with the personal year cycle which is derived from your month and day of birth.

Despite their differences, most numerical symbologies follow the same basic pattern of progression. Each successive number represents another dimension of the life process; in their totality, numbers cover the entire spectrum of human experience within the life cycle of man. Thus, for example, the number 1 represents man alone—the divine spark, the beginning, the self, the pioneer. Then comes woman, the number 2, representing union, marriage, togetherness, sharing. 1 and 2 join together to form the number 3, representative of self-expression, fruitfulness, birth. With the number 4, man turns his attention to building a home. He learns about self-discipline, limitations and endurance. Then, his labor accomplished, he is ready for a diversion. The number 5 brings change, curiosity, freedom, awareness of the sensual aspects of life. 6 represents the development of social consciousness; working with and adjusting to the needs of others in both family and community. 7 introduces intellectual and spiritual development, faith and belief in a higher power. With 8 there is a return to work and an emphasis on material accomplishment and power. Finally we get to the number 9—universal love, awareness, selflessness, humanitarian goals and breadth of philosophy.

*The following books are presently available from Newcastle Publishing Co.: Seton, Julia, M.D., *Symbols of Numerology* (1984) and Jordan, Juno and Helen Houston, *Your Name/Your Number/Your Destiny* (1982).

Finding Your Guide Numbers

As you can see, the odd numbers (1, 3, 5, 7, 9) are more related to thoughts and ideas, whereas the even numbers (2, 4, 6, 8) stress life's practical realities. As stated in Shakespeare's *The Merry Wives of Windsor*: "There is divinity in odd numbers, either in nativity, chance or death."

Some key words you may want to become familier with for the numbers 1 through 9 include the following:

	POSITIVE	NEGATIVE
1	independence initiative decisiveness	selfishness egotism loneliness
2	union partnership details	depression oversensitivity pettiness
3	communication beauty social activity	scattered energy vanity extravagance
4	routine structure security	inflexibility narrow-mindedness overwork or laziness
5	freedom change physical senses	overindulgence irresponsibility recklessness
6	responsibility domesticity service to others	stubborness meddlesomeness worry
7	wisdom specialization research	aloofness escapism withdrawal
8	executive ability big business organization	greed misuse of authority poor judgment
9	humanitarianism universality charisma	possessiveness jealousy overemotionalism

Your Daily Numerology

Many people wonder whether there are "good" numbers and "bad" numbers? "Is it *good* to be a 1?" "Is it *bad* to be a 5?" There are no numbers that are better or worse than any other. There are only numbers that are "different." All numbers have a positive and a negative vibration. All numbers are good if you take advantage of their strengths. If you catch yourself working on the weaknesses, however, you can discipline yourself consciously to change.

For example, let's say you're in a 3 personal year and you find you're spending too much money shopping, eating out and on frivolous extras. If you know that you are experiencing the influence of the 3 vibration, you know that you have a tendency now to be extravagant and scatter your energy. Yes, 3 is social and you should pamper yourself and have a good time, but *within reason*! Don't let all self-discipline go out the window. Again, work with the positive.

Even the numbers that aren't on your chart have something important to say. The numerical values which are absent in your birth chart stand for the lessons you are here to learn on your evolutionary path of growth toward a higher level of being. They provide insights into the reasons why you are living this particular life and what you will have to contend with here. Since everyone has different lessons to learn, what is easy for one person may be difficult for another, and vice versa. Of one thing, however, you can be certain: you will always attract to yourself those experiences that are necessary for your inner development—over that you have no choice. Where your free will comes into play is in how you deal with these situations. Changing the way you perceive and handle them will, in turn, change the way you experience them.

Very often difficulties arise through poor timing. The purpose of this book, then, is to show you how to find out what forces are influencing you and what they mean, so you will be better equipped to deal with them. By knowing what to expect in advance, you can prepare yourself to take advantage of the opportunities and avoid the pitfalls. Instead of stumbling through life at the mercy of the various events and conditions surrounding you, you can be the creator of what you wish to experience.

Chapter One will show you how to find your own personal guide numbers. By showing you which times are most harmoni-

Finding Your Guide Numbers

ous for doing certain things, and which times are likely to present the most difficulties, the daily forecasts that follow can help you make the most out of every month and day of each year. Use them as a road map to help you plan ahead. Let your numbers be your guide.

CHAPTER ONE

FINDING YOUR GUIDE NUMBERS

There are three daily guide numbers—one corresponding to the vibration of your personal year, one corresponding to your personal month and one corresponding to your personal day. However, all you really have to know is your personal year. We have done all the rest of the work for you. Consult the table at the end of this chapter, or calculate your personal year according to the following instructions.

To find out what personal year of the nine-year cycle you happen to be in at present is very simple. Just add up the *month* you were born, the *day* you were born, and the *present calendar year*. Then reduce the sum of these three numbers to a single digit. This digit is also your guide number for the year.

For example, if you were born on August 6, and the present year is 1987, then 1987 will be a 3 personal year and your guide number will be 3:

      8 (August is the 8th month of the year)
      6 (calendar day)
+ 1987 (calendar year)
   2001 = (2 + 0 + 0 + 1) = 21 (2 + 1) = 3

Or, if you were born on October 15, then 1987 will be a 5 personal year and your guide number will be 5:

Your Daily Numerology

```
    10   (October is the 10th month of the year)
    15   (calendar day)
+ 1987   (calendar year)
  2012 = (2 + 0 + 1 + 2) = 5
```

and so on.

That is all there is to it! You are now ready to refer to the chapter that corresponds to your personal year. There you will find guide numbers and forecasts for every month and day from January 1 through December 31.*

You will notice that each year also has a color associated with it. By wearing the color of your personal year or by having it around, even in a small item, you will attract vibrations harmonious to your special cycle.

---

*For those who are curious about how we get the other two guide numbers, we offer the following explanation: The second guide number, your personal month, is found by adding your personal year to the present calendar month. For example, if you are in a 7 personal year, May is a 3 personal month: 7 + 5 (May is the fifth month of the year) = 12 (1 + 2) = 3.

The third guide number, your personal day, is found by adding your personal month to the calendar day. For example, if you are in a 3 personal month, the 16th of that month is a 1 personal day: 3 + 16 = 19 (19) = 10 (1 + 0) = 1.

PERSONAL YEAR

BIRTHDAY	1986	1987	1988	1989	1990	1991	1992	1993	1994	1995	1996	1997	1998	1999	2000	2001	2002	2003
JAN 1,10,19,28	8	9	1	2	3	4	5	6	7	8	9	1	2	3	4	5	6	7
JAN 2,11,20,29	9	1	2	3	4	5	6	7	8	9	1	2	3	4	5	6	7	8
JAN 3,12,21,30	1	2	3	4	5	6	7	8	9	1	2	3	4	5	6	7	8	9
JAN 4,13,22,31	2	3	4	5	6	7	8	9	1	2	3	4	5	6	7	8	9	1
JAN 5,14,23	3	4	5	6	7	8	9	1	2	3	4	5	6	7	8	9	1	2
JAN 6,15,24	4	5	6	7	8	9	1	2	3	4	5	6	7	8	9	1	2	3
JAN 7,16,25	5	6	7	8	9	1	2	3	4	5	6	7	8	9	1	2	3	4
JAN 8,17,26	6	7	8	9	1	2	3	4	5	6	7	8	9	1	2	3	4	5
JAN 9,18,27	7	8	9	1	2	3	4	5	6	7	8	9	1	2	3	4	5	6
FEB 1,10,19,28	9	1	2	3	4	5	6	7	8	9	1	2	3	4	5	6	7	8
FEB 2,11,20,29	1	2	3	4	5	6	7	8	9	1	2	3	4	5	6	7	8	9
FEB 3,12,21	2	3	4	5	6	7	8	9	1	2	3	4	5	6	7	8	9	1
FEB 4,13,22	3	4	5	6	7	8	9	1	2	3	4	5	6	7	8	9	1	2
FEB 5,14,23	4	5	6	7	8	9	1	2	3	4	5	6	7	8	9	1	2	3
FEB 6,15,24	5	6	7	8	9	1	2	3	4	5	6	7	8	9	1	2	3	4
FEB 7,16,25	6	7	8	9	1	2	3	4	5	6	7	8	9	1	2	3	4	5
FEB 8,17,26	7	8	9	1	2	3	4	5	6	7	8	9	1	2	3	4	5	6
FEB 9,18,27	8	9	1	2	3	4	5	6	7	8	9	1	2	3	4	5	6	7
MAR 1,10,19,28	1	2	3	4	5	6	7	8	9	1	2	3	4	5	6	7	8	9
MAR 2,11,20,29	2	3	4	5	6	7	8	9	1	2	3	4	5	6	7	8	9	1
MAR 3,12,21,30	3	4	5	6	7	8	9	1	2	3	4	5	6	7	8	9	1	2

Find your birthday in the lefthand column and read across to the current year column. The number where the two columns meet is your Personal Year. Go to that chapter to find your guide numbers.

BIRTHDAY	1986	1987	1988	1989	1990	1991	1992	1993	1994	1995	1996	1997	1998	1999	2000	2001	2002	2003
MAR 4,13,22,31	4	5	6	7	8	9	1	2	3	4	5	6	7	8	9	1	2	3
MAR 5,14,23	5	6	7	8	9	1	2	3	4	5	6	7	8	9	1	2	3	4
MAR 6,15,24	6	7	8	9	1	2	3	4	5	6	7	8	9	1	2	3	4	5
MAR 7,16,25	7	8	9	1	2	3	4	5	6	7	8	9	1	2	3	4	5	6
MAR 8,17,26	8	9	1	2	3	4	5	6	7	8	9	1	2	3	4	5	6	7
MAR 9,18,27	9	1	2	3	4	5	6	7	8	9	1	2	3	4	5	6	7	8
APR 1,10,19,28	2	3	4	5	6	7	8	9	1	2	3	4	5	6	7	8	9	1
APR 2,11,20,29	3	4	5	6	7	8	9	1	2	3	4	5	6	7	8	9	1	2
APR 3,12,21,30	4	5	6	7	8	9	1	2	3	4	5	6	7	8	9	1	2	3
APR 4,13,22	5	6	7	8	9	1	2	3	4	5	6	7	8	9	1	2	3	4
APR 5,14,23	6	7	8	9	1	2	3	4	5	6	7	8	9	1	2	3	4	5
APR 6,15,24	7	8	9	1	2	3	4	5	6	7	8	9	1	2	3	4	5	6
APR 7,16,25	8	9	1	2	3	4	5	6	7	8	9	1	2	3	4	5	6	7
APR 8,17,26	9	1	2	3	4	5	6	7	8	9	1	2	3	4	5	6	7	8
APR 9,18,27	1	2	3	4	5	6	7	8	9	1	2	3	4	5	6	7	8	9
MAY 1,10,19,28	3	4	5	6	7	8	9	1	2	3	4	5	6	7	8	9	1	2
MAY 2,11,20,29	4	5	6	7	8	9	1	2	3	4	5	6	7	8	9	1	2	3
MAY 3,12,21,30	5	6	7	8	9	1	2	3	4	5	6	7	8	9	1	2	3	4
MAY 4,13,22,31	6	7	8	9	1	2	3	4	5	6	7	8	9	1	2	3	4	5
MAY 5,14,23	7	8	9	1	2	3	4	5	6	7	8	9	1	2	3	4	5	6

Find your birthday in the lefthand column and read across to the current year column. The number where the two columns meet is your Personal Year. Go to that chapter to find your guide numbers.

Birthday																						
MAY 6,15,24	7	8	9	1	3	4	5	6	7	8	9	1	2	4	5	6	7	8	9	1	2	3
MAY 7,16,25	6	7	8	9	2	3	4	5	6	7	8	9	1	3	4	5	6	7	8	9	1	2
MAY 8,17,26	5	6	7	8	1	2	3	4	5	6	7	8	9	2	3	4	5	6	7	8	9	1
MAY 9,18,27	4	5	6	7	9	1	2	3	4	5	6	7	8	1	2	3	4	5	6	7	8	9
JUNE 1,10,19,28	3	4	5	6	8	9	1	2	3	4	5	6	7	9	1	2	3	4	5	6	7	8
JUNE 2,11,20,29	2	3	4	5	7	8	9	1	2	3	4	5	6	8	9	1	2	3	4	5	6	7
JUNE 3,12,21,30	1	2	3	4	6	7	8	9	1	2	3	4	5	7	8	9	1	2	3	4	5	6
JUNE 4,13,22	9	1	2	3	5	6	7	8	9	1	2	3	4	6	7	8	9	1	2	3	4	5
JUNE 5,14,23	8	9	1	2	4	5	6	7	8	9	1	2	3	5	6	7	8	9	1	2	3	4
JUNE 6,15,24	7	8	9	1	3	4	5	6	7	8	9	1	2	4	5	6	7	8	9	1	2	3
JUNE 7,16,25	6	7	8	9	2	3	4	5	6	7	8	9	1	3	4	5	6	7	8	9	1	2
JUNE 8,17,26	5	6	7	8	1	2	3	4	5	6	7	8	9	2	3	4	5	6	7	8	9	1
JUNE 9,18,27	4	5	6	7	9	1	2	3	4	5	6	7	8	1	2	3	4	5	6	7	8	9
JULY 1,10,19,28	3	4	5	6	8	9	1	2	3	4	5	6	7	9	1	2	3	4	5	6	7	8
JULY 2,11,20,29	2	3	4	5	7	8	9	1	2	3	4	5	6	8	9	1	2	3	4	5	6	7
JULY 3,12,21,30	1	2	3	4	6	7	8	9	1	2	3	4	5	7	8	9	1	2	3	4	5	6
JULY 4,13,22,31	9	1	2	3	5	6	7	8	9	1	2	3	4	6	7	8	9	1	2	3	4	5
JULY 5,14,23	8	9	1	2	4	5	6	7	8	9	1	2	3	5	6	7	8	9	1	2	3	4
JULY 6,15,24	7	8	9	1	3	4	5	6	7	8	9	1	2	4	5	6	7	8	9	1	2	3
JULY 7,16,25	6	7	8	9	2	3	4	5	6	7	8	9	1	3	4	5	6	7	8	9	1	2
JULY 8,17,26	5	6	7	8	1	2	3	4	5	6	7	8	9	2	3	4	5	6	7	8	9	1
JULY 9,18,27	4	5	6	7	9	1	2	3	4	5	6	7	8	1	2	3	4	5	6	7	8	9

Find your birthday in the lefthand column and read across to the current year column. The number where the two columns meet is your Personal Year. Go to that chapter to find your guide numbers.

BIRTHDAY	1986	1987	1988	1989	1990	1991	1992	1993	1994	1995	1996	1997	1998	1999	2000	2001	2002	2003
AUG 1,10,19,28	6	7	8	9	1	2	3	4	5	6	7	8	9	1	2	3	4	5
AUG 2,11,20,29	7	8	9	1	2	3	4	5	6	7	8	9	1	2	3	4	5	6
AUG 3,12,21,30	8	9	1	2	3	4	5	6	7	8	9	1	2	3	4	5	6	7
AUG 4,13,22,31	9	1	2	3	4	5	6	7	8	9	1	2	3	4	5	6	7	8
AUG 5,14,23	1	2	3	4	5	6	7	8	9	1	2	3	4	5	6	7	8	9
AUG 6,15,24	2	3	4	5	6	7	8	9	1	2	3	4	5	6	7	8	9	1
AUG 7,16,25	3	4	5	6	7	8	9	1	2	3	4	5	6	7	8	9	1	2
AUG 8,17,26	4	5	6	7	8	9	1	2	3	4	5	6	7	8	9	1	2	3
AUG 9,18,27	5	6	7	8	9	1	2	3	4	5	6	7	8	9	1	2	3	4
SEPT 1,10,19,28	7	8	9	1	2	3	4	5	6	7	8	9	1	2	3	4	5	6
SEPT 2,11,20,29	8	9	1	2	3	4	5	6	7	8	9	1	2	3	4	5	6	7
SEPT 3,12,21,30	9	1	2	3	4	5	6	7	8	9	1	2	3	4	5	6	7	8
SEPT 4,13,22	1	2	3	4	5	6	7	8	9	1	2	3	4	5	6	7	8	9
SEPT 5,14,23	2	3	4	5	6	7	8	9	1	2	3	4	5	6	7	8	9	1
SEPT 6,15,24	3	4	5	6	7	8	9	1	2	3	4	5	6	7	8	9	1	2
SEPT 7,16,25	4	5	6	7	8	9	1	2	3	4	5	6	7	8	9	1	2	3
SEPT 8,17,26	5	6	7	8	9	1	2	3	4	5	6	7	8	9	1	2	3	4
SEPT 9,18,27	6	7	8	9	1	2	3	4	5	6	7	8	9	1	2	3	4	5
OCT 1,10,19,28	8	9	1	2	3	4	5	6	7	8	9	1	2	3	4	5	6	7
OCT 2,11,20,29	9	1	2	3	4	5	6	7	8	9	1	2	3	4	5	6	7	8
OCT 3,12,21,30	1	2	3	4	5	6	7	8	9	1	2	3	4	5	6	7	8	9
OCT 4,13,22,31	2	3	4	5	6	7	8	9	1	2	3	4	5	6	7	8	9	1

Find your birthday in the lefthand column and read across to the current year column. The number where the two columns meet is your Personal Year. Go to that chapter to find your guide numbers.

Date																			
OCT 5,14,23	2	3	4	5	6	7	8	9	1	2	3	4	5	6	7	8	9	1	2
OCT 6,15,24	3	4	5	6	7	8	9	1	2	3	4	5	6	7	8	9	1	2	3
OCT 7,16,25	4	5	6	7	8	9	1	2	3	4	5	6	7	8	9	1	2	3	4
OCT 8,17,26	5	6	7	8	9	1	2	3	4	5	6	7	8	9	1	2	3	4	5
OCT 9,18,27	6	7	8	9	1	2	3	4	5	6	7	8	9	1	2	3	4	5	6
NOV 1,10,19,28	8	9	1	2	3	4	5	6	7	8	9	1	2	3	4	5	6	7	8
NOV 2,11,20,29	9	1	2	3	4	5	6	7	8	9	1	2	3	4	5	6	7	8	9
NOV 3,12,21,30	1	2	3	4	5	6	7	8	9	1	2	3	4	5	6	7	8	9	1
NOV 4,13,22	2	3	4	5	6	7	8	9	1	2	3	4	5	6	7	8	9	1	2
NOV 5,14,23	3	4	5	6	7	8	9	1	2	3	4	5	6	7	8	9	1	2	3
NOV 6,15,24	4	5	6	7	8	9	1	2	3	4	5	6	7	8	9	1	2	3	4
NOV 7,16,25	5	6	7	8	9	1	2	3	4	5	6	7	8	9	1	2	3	4	5
NOV 8,17,26	6	7	8	9	1	2	3	4	5	6	7	8	9	1	2	3	4	5	6
NOV 9,18,27	7	8	9	1	2	3	4	5	6	7	8	9	1	2	3	4	5	6	7
DEC 1,10,19,28	9	1	2	3	4	5	6	7	8	9	1	2	3	4	5	6	7	8	9
DEC 2,11,20,29	1	2	3	4	5	6	7	8	9	1	2	3	4	5	6	7	8	9	1
DEC 3,12,21,30	2	3	4	5	6	7	8	9	1	2	3	4	5	6	7	8	9	1	2
DEC 4,13,22,31	3	4	5	6	7	8	9	1	2	3	4	5	6	7	8	9	1	2	3
DEC 5,14,23	4	5	6	7	8	9	1	2	3	4	5	6	7	8	9	1	2	3	4
DEC 6,15,24	5	6	7	8	9	1	2	3	4	5	6	7	8	9	1	2	3	4	5
DEC 7,16,25	6	7	8	9	1	2	3	4	5	6	7	8	9	1	2	3	4	5	6
DEC 8,17,26	7	8	9	1	2	3	4	5	6	7	8	9	1	2	3	4	5	6	7
DEC 9,18,27	8	9	1	2	3	4	5	6	7	8	9	1	2	3	4	5	6	7	8

Find your birthday in the lefthand column and read across to the current year column. The number where the two columns meet is your Personal Year. Go to that chapter to find your guide numbers.

CHAPTER TWO

THE 1 YEAR

"Planting the Seeds"

GUIDE NUMBER: 1
COLOR: RED

This is the year for new beginnings—the year that sets the tone for the whole nine-year cycle to follow. It is the time to plant seeds—the more the better. Unless you plant seeds there can be no harvest. Get the ball rolling, start something new—change jobs, move, seek that raise or promotion, make new friends, get involved in a hobby. Whatever you initiate is practically guaranteed success. But one word of caution: good judgment is a must! The things you start now, whether good or bad, are likely to be around for a long time, and so friendships, especially, should be chosen with care.

You will probably be feeling more energetic, assertive and aggressive than usual and should use these forces to your advantage. Be self-reliant, confident and willing to take the lead or make the plunge. Strike out on your own and don't let others hold you back or interfere with your plans. Success and happiness come from being independent, creative, positive, selective and following your own intuition and instincts. Avoid lack of initiative, which may result in floundering that will continue throughout the entire nine-year cycle.

Your Daily Numerology

JANUARY
Guide Numbers: 1, 2

Patience and cooperation are the keynotes to success and happiness this month. Although delays and/or people who fail to live up to your expectations may be a source of frustration, don't push for action right now. Try not to be impulsive but look carefully into details. Listen to what others have to say.

January 1st, 10th, 19th, 28th
Guide Numbers: 1, 2, 3

This is a good day to explore new interests—that class in flower arranging or auto mechanics, perhaps. Social events are a source of pleasure, and a new person who enters your life may wind up being a romantic partner or business contact.

January 2nd, 11th, 20th, 29th
Guide Numbers: 1, 2, 4

You may feel bogged down by unrelenting tedium. Do your necessary work, but take time out to spend with family or friends. Without taking on more than your share, offer help and understanding to those who depend on you.

January 3rd, 12th, 21st, 30th
Guide Numbers: 1, 2, 5

You are full of restless energy and have a need to be physically active. Take care, however, as you rush from place to place, not to stub your toe, get a speeding ticket or lose your temper over having to wait in line at the store.

January 4th, 13th, 22nd, 31st
Guide Numbers: 1, 2, 6

Spend the day with loved ones or friends. Be patient when someone needs a shoulder to lean on and try to lend a sympathetic ear—you may want the favor returned some day.

January 5th, 14th, 23rd
Guide Numbers: 1, 2, 7

The 1 Year: Planting the Seeds

This is a good day for mental and spiritual pursuits. Try not to let petty annoyances get you down. Changing negative thoughts into positive ones could result in a pleasant experience.

January 6th, 15th, 24th
Guide Numbers: 1, 2, 8
   Don't let your emotions rule your head. It's okay to seek advice from an expert about a decision you have to make, but don't expect him or her to make up your mind for you. Be prepared to act on your own.

January 7th, 16th, 25th
Guide Numbers: 1, 2, 9
   This is a good day to finish up that project you've been working on with a friend. Try to remain objective and calm on the job. A journey may sound appealing but make sure it's worth the cost.

January 8th, 17th, 26th
Guide Numbers: 1, 2, 1
   Put the past behind you and dwell on the present. New projects may require your cooperation with others, but the final decision should be yours. Try to avoid headstrong tactics that could discourage someone new from entering your life.

January 9th, 18th, 27th
Guide Numbers: 1, 2, 2
   Patience and tact may be needed today as you are forced to cooperate with others on something you feel you could do better and faster by yourself. Try to be appreciative of friends and loved ones.

FEBRUARY
Guide Numbers: 1, 3
   Friends play an important part in this month's events. Self-expression and sociability pay off now, but try not to get carried away by enthusiasm or talk too much about your plans. Careless words and impulsive actions are likely to be regretted later on. Buy yourself something new and take steps to improve your appearance.

Your Daily Numerology

February 1st, 10th, 19th, 28th
Guide Numbers: 1, 3, 4

This is a day when practical decisions need to be made, such as whether to go to the dentist or start looking for a new job, whether to redecorate the den or pay off a loan. Although you may be faced with mundane frustrations, try not to let them get you down.

February 2nd, 11th, 20th, 29th
Guide Numbers: 1, 3, 5

You may hear some unexpected news or have an opportunity to take a short trip. Gossip and phone calls take up much of your time and could interfere with your work.

February 3rd, 12th, 21st
Guide Numbers: 1, 3, 6

Domestic activities are highlighted; you may find yourself spending more time in the kitchen than usual. Someone close needs your emotional support, and you could have some added responsibility, possibly involving a child.

February 4th, 13th, 22nd
Guide Numbers: 1, 3, 7

Don't take anything at face value now—there may be more to a rumor or situation than meets the eye. This is a good day to write letters, meet with close friends or expand your knowledge in some way. Something you see or hear may capture your interest.

February 5th, 14th, 23rd
Guide Numbers: 1, 3, 8

Social contacts you make can help you get ahead in your career. Don't be afraid to say what's on your mind or ask for what you want, but make sure you use good judgment and avoid sounding arrogant or headstrong.

February 6th, 15th, 24th
Guide Numbers: 1, 3, 9

Self-expression is highlighted; your mind is more likely to be on social or creative activities or having a good time than on mundane tasks such as scrubbing floors. Be discreet when discussing sensitive subjects.

The 1 Year: Planting the Seeds

February 7th, 16th, 25th
Guide Numbers: 1, 3, 1
  Energy and optimism are high, but try not to get carried away by enthusiasm or talk too much about your personal life or plans. A new friendship could lead to romance.

February 8th, 17th, 26th
Guide Numbers: 1, 3, 2
  You may have some extra responsibility due to a friend's need, but it should not be a burden for you. In fact, it could be something you enjoy. A romantic interlude may be a source of pleasure.

February 9th, 18th, 27th
Guide Numbers: 1, 3, 3
  This is a good day to socialize; you are likely to be in the limelight at some time. Don't leave the house looking like a wreck because you're only going to the supermarket or taking the garbage out. That's just the time you could bump into someone important.

MARCH
Guide Numbers: 1, 4
  Practical matters need to be taken care of now, and you may feel irritable and resentful when they require more of your time than you are willing to spare. You are also likely to feel restricted or disappointed in some way. Proper diet, adequate rest and some tension-ridding activity are essential to your well-being.

March 1st, 10th, 19th, 28th
Guide Numbers: 1, 4, 5
  Something unexpected will happen: perhaps someone will offer you a free theater ticket, your gas and electric bill may turn out to be a lot more than you expected, or you may bump into an old friend on the bus. Don't let your mind wander at an inappropriate time.

March 2nd, 11th, 20th, 29th
Guide Numbers: 1, 4, 6

Your Daily Numerology

An understanding attitude and a willingness to adjust help keep a relationship running smoothly. You may need to discharge some responsibility before you can tend to your own interests, but don't lose your temper because of it.

March 3rd, 12th, 21st, 30th
Guide Numbers: 1, 4, 7

This is a good day for study, writing or learning a skill. You can accomplish a great deal provided you don't let minor delays or irritations interrupt your train of thought.

March 4th, 13th, 22nd, 31st
Guide Numbers: 1, 4, 8

You are at your most efficient and can get a lot done both at home and at work. It is a good time to attend to practical, down-to-earth matters, whether these are going for a job interview, organizing closets or outlining a report.

March 5th, 14th, 23rd
Guide Numbers: 1, 4, 9

You might find yourself getting together with an old acquaintance or business associate. Maintain a broad outlook if you're presented with a lifestyle other than your own.

March 6th, 15th, 24th
Guide Numbers: 1, 4, 1

You may feel discouraged by all the work you have to do. Take it step by step and have faith that your efforts will pay off. This is a good day to apply yourself to building a foundation for future security.

March 7th, 16th, 25th
Guide Numbers: 1, 4, 2

Don't expect things to happen too fast. It's a time to take care of details and do those little chores that have to be done *some* time. You'll be happiest if you have a chance to work and share with others.

March 8th, 17th, 26th
Guide Numbers: 1, 4, 3

The 1 Year: Planting the Seeds

Meeting a friend can provide a refreshing pause in the midst of a busy day. You'll want to catch up on the news and may spend a lot of time on the phone. A shopping spree would do you good, but take care not to go overboard.

March 9th, 18th, 27th
Guide Numbers: 1, 4, 4
You're rooted in structure and routine and may have a tendency to be a bit rigid or stubborn. Although it's a day for hard work and self-discipline, you should maintain an optimistic outlook and a sense of humor.

APRIL
Guide Numbers: 1, 5
Opportunity comes your way: there could be some changes in your home situation or job. New interests open new doors, but you may feel some uncertainty as to which direction to take. Be adaptable to disruptions in your daily routine. This is a month full of unexpected surprises which will test your resourcefulness. A short trip is likely.

April 1st, 10th, 19th, 28th
Guide Numbers: 1, 5, 6
Duties and responsibilities could interfere with your desire to do your own thing, and adjustments will have to be made. Try not to get too involved with other people's problems or talk too much about your own.

April 2nd, 11th, 20th, 29th
Guide Numbers: 1, 5, 7
If you've felt burdened by routine work lately, you'll be especially restless. A long walk could help renew your spirits. Good things may come your way if you are receptive and willing to accept challenges.

April 3rd, 12th, 21st, 30th
Guide Numbers: 1, 5, 8

Your Daily Numerology

Use good judgment when signing papers or attending to a legal matter. A proposal of some sort which is financially beneficial to you may come through. Be open to new experiences that can give your life a broader scope.

April 4th, 13th, 22nd
Guide Numbers: 1, 5, 9

This is a good time for dealing with the public or participating in school or club activities. Romance is likely to be on your mind, and you may be distracted by your daydreams when you should be concentrating on something important. Write things down rather than depend on your memory.

April 5th, 14th, 23rd
Guide Numbers: 1, 5, 1

Forge ahead, promote yourself and go after what you want. There may be so many new avenues to explore that you feel confused as to which to take advantage of. Once you decide on what you want to do, act without delay.

April 6th, 15th, 24th
Guide Numbers: 1, 5, 2

You have much to gain by working and sharing with others. Your patience may be tested by someone who is difficult to deal with, but you can avoid an upsetting situation by handling the matter with tact and diplomacy.

April 7th, 16th, 25th
Guide Numbers: 1, 5, 3

You are likely to be in a social mood and may have a hard time keeping your mind on work. Get out and mingle and do something you enjoy. This is a good time for meeting people.

April 8th, 17th, 26th
Guide Numbers: 1, 5, 4

This is a day to work hard on any changes you want to make in your life. If you keep your mind on the task at hand, you are likely to accomplish even more than you thought possible. You may meet someone interesting who supports your ideas.

The 1 Year: Planting the Seeds

April 9th, 18th, 27th
Guide Numbers: 1, 5, 5
Unexpected things crop up to test your resourcefulness and adaptability. You may be anxious for change and feel restless for no apparent reason at all. A new person who enters your life could be quite influential later on.

MAY
Guide Numbers: 1, 6
Responsibility to others may prevent you from spending as much time as you'd like on your own projects this month. Those close to you seek sympathy and advice and make many demands on your time. Although you have strong opinions about what is right or wrong, try to be understanding and open-minded. Compromise and adjustment are the keynotes to success and happiness. Resentment is detrimental to your health.

May 1st, 10th, 19th, 28th
Guide Numbers: 1, 6, 7
You are likely to be feeling some uncertainty. Make sure you analyze a situation well and look beneath the surface before jumping to conclusions. Don't let boredom or loneliness get you down. Exploring a study or idea that interests you can be inspiring and uplifting.

May 2nd, 11th, 20th, 29th
Guide Numbers: 1, 6, 8
You may learn something of value from someone you meet. A pet or family member could need your special attention, and you may have to juggle your schedule around to accommodate the situation.

May 3rd, 12th, 21st, 30th
Guide Numbers: 1, 6, 9
A combination of frustrations that have been allowed to build up could lead to angry, jealous or resentful feelings. Even though you may not be able to pinpoint their cause, try to cleanse

yourself of these negative emotions. Count your blessings and concentrate on making your life work.

May 4th, 13th, 22nd, 31st
Guide Numbers: 1, 6, 1
New beginnings are in the air and this is a good time to tackle a responsibility that comes your way. Others may seek your help and advice, and although there is much you want to do, some adjustments will have to be made to the needs of those who are close to you.

May 5th, 14th, 23rd
Guide Numbers: 1, 6, 2
Small details are likely to be the focus of your attention. You may soon be so concerned about having whatever you are working on turn out just right that you'll be tempted to tell others how things should be done. It's okay to assert yourself, but do it in a tactful, diplomatic way.

May 6th, 15th, 24th
Guide Numbers: 1, 6, 3
You'll feel like being with friends, but you'll want it to be on your terms. Make sure communications are clear, so as to avoid misunderstandings. Words flow freely and you must take care not to be opinionated or become involved in gossip.

May 7th, 16th, 25th
Guide Numbers: 1, 6, 4
Apply yourself to the tasks at hand. Although having to work hard may not seem appealing, you'll see pleasing results at a later date. If you have been considering a move or a home improvement of some kind, this is a good time to make it.

May 8th, 17th, 26th
Guide Numbers: 1, 6, 5
An unexpected matter concerning a family member could come up. Be adaptable to changes in your schedule. The principle of a thing could be an issue now, and you may find yourself defending your position.

The 1 Year: Planting the Seeds

May 9th, 18th, 27th
Guide Numbers: 1, 6, 6
 Domestic and business responsibilities are likely to keep you busy. You could be anxious about winning an argument to prove you're right, but try to avoid sounding overbearing. A family dinner may be the highlight of the day.

JUNE
Guide Numbers: 1, 7
 Think, analyze and perfect your ideas, but wait until next month to put them into action. Although delays are upsetting, attempts to force issues of a business or financial nature are likely to be disappointing. Mental pursuits are favored, and this is a good time to take up some study of an inspiring or uplifting nature.

June 1st, 10th, 19th, 28th
Guide Numbers: 1, 7, 8
 Improving your mind is one way of gaining more independence and control, and printed matter may be of special interest to you. This is a good time to think about how you could become more efficient on your job and to work toward career advancement.

June 2nd, 11th, 20th, 29th
Guide Numbers: 1, 7, 9
 Something you've been waiting for could come through; you are likely to experience a feeling of relief as a situation or project comes to an end. Others may look to you for guidance.

June 3rd, 12th, 21st, 30th
Guide Numbers: 1, 7, 1
 You may feel like being alone and would be happier working on your own, or at least without someone constantly looking over your shoulder. Solitude breeds creativity, and you are likely to find interruptions or idle chit-chat irritating.

Your Daily Numerology

June 4th, 13th, 22nd
Guide Numbers: 1, 7, 2
    It's better to take your time and do your work thoroughly and accurately rather than attempt to rush through it. Use caution if you must make an important decision and don't take anything at face value. Patience and tact will pay off.

June 5th, 14th, 23rd
Guide Numbers: 1, 7, 3
    This is a good time to go to a lecture or discussion group on some topic that interests you. Self-expression is highlighted, and you will want to talk with others who share your interests. However, try to avod becoming involved in idle gossip.

June 6th, 15th, 24th
Guide Numbers: 1, 7, 4
    Practical matters demand your attention, and you may resent not having enough time for yourself. Try to take minor irritations in stride and focus on long-term goals.

June 7th, 16th, 25th
Guide Numbers: 1, 7, 5
    News from an unexpected source may lead you to consider a trip you hadn't planned on. Before making a hasty decision, however, make sure you can afford it—in terms of both time and finances.

June 8th, 17th, 26th
Guide Numbers: 1, 7, 6
    You could find certain family members annoying. If possible, plan to be with only those people you get along with well. There will undoubtedly be some person or situation you'll have to adjust to.

June 9th, 18th, 27th
Guide Numbers: 1, 7, 7
    You may have a strong desire to get away from it all and seek some form of escape: retreating to your room with a book, taking a long drive or drinking yourself into a stupor. Your physical energy is at a low, so be sure you get enough rest.

The 1 Year: Planting the Seeds

JULY
Guide Numbers: 1, 8

Initiative is the keynote to success and happiness this month and you should avoid indecision or inertia. This is a time to get out and do the things you have been thinking about doing for a while. Finances could be a little tight, but efficiency and good judgment pay off. A promotion or a business-connected trip or move is possible.

July 1st, 10th, 19th, 28th
Guide Numbers: 1, 8, 9

Today is likely to be filled with activity. You may have an experience which will inspire you to look at things from a broader perspective, or at least to consider something you would never have before. Forge ahead with your plans, but show some compassion for others too.

July 2nd, 11th, 20th, 29th
Guide Numbers: 1, 8, 1

This is a good time for a business trip or meeting. Your self-confidence and determination should be high, making this the perfect time to act on your ideas. If the cleverest ones are followed up, they could lead to an increase in income.

July 3rd, 12th, 21st, 30th
Guide Numbers: 1, 8, 2

New ventures are on the horizon. Some may be only stepping-stones or momentary diversions, others could last a lifetime. You will gain from your associations with others and from listening to sound advice.

July 4th, 13th, 22nd, 31st
Guide Numbers: 1, 8, 3

Communications are highlighted and you are likely to spend more time than usual talking on the phone. Social contacts could be significant and lead to a new opportunity in your career.

July 5th, 14th, 23rd
Guide Numbers: 1, 8, 4

Your Daily Numerology

You may feel bogged down by work or routine and not know quite how to break the monotony. Even if you're on vacation you may be confused as to what activities would be the most fun. Money could be an issue and some expenditures may not seem worth the price.

July 6th, 15th, 24th
Guide Numbers: 1, 8, 5

You may find yourself taking a chance on something that you ordinarily wouldn't, or striking off in a new direction where your career is concerned. Make sure you are alert to whatever is to your best advantage before choosing a course of action.

July 7th, 16th, 25th
Guide Numbers: 1, 8, 6

You must take your responsibilities seriously. Even if you're on vacation or at some festive occasion, be aware of where you are and whom you're dealing with and act accordingly. If you plan wisely now, you can be of assistance to someone who needs your help without having to cancel any of your own plans.

July 8th, 17th, 26th
Guide Numbers: 1, 8, 7

Today is a day to think, plan, observe and analyze. Idle chatter is likely to irritate you, as more important things are on your mind. Being by yourself for a while to rest or study would be beneficial.

July 9th, 18th, 27th
Guide Numbers: 1, 8, 8

You should have no trouble making decisions or managing your affairs. Although others may look to you for leadership or advice, you are unlikely to feel burdened by their dependence on you. Act now if you think the time is right.

AUGUST
Guide Numbers: 1, 9

Love, understanding and humanitarian interests are the keynotes for happiness this month. This is a good time to undertake

The 1 Year: Planting the Seeds

some study or activity that will expand your perspective. Results long delayed start to be seen, and you are likely to experience a change in feelings. Put your creative energy to use.

August 1st, 10th, 19th, 28th
Guide Numbers: 1, 9, 1

Don't depend on anyone else to solve your problems. This is a time to stand on your own two feet and act alone. Although you may be feeling impatient, on edge, or easily irritated by the actions of others, don't jump to hasty conclusions.

August 2nd, 11th, 20th, 29th
Guide Numbers: 1, 9, 2

Interaction with others is highlighted, and you will need to be selective in regard to how you spend your time. Be patient, find a positive outlet for your nervous energy and tackle daily problems with objectivity and the determination that they won't get you down.

August 3rd, 12th, 21st, 30th
Guide Numbers: 1, 9, 3

Communications are highlighted, and you may find yourself doing anything from writing letters to visiting with friends. Take care not to scatter your energies in too many directions or you could wear yourself out.

August 4th, 13th, 22nd, 31st
Guide Numbers: 1, 9, 4

Applying yourself to your chores may take more of an effort than usual. You may resent having some new responsibility, but in all likelihood if will only be a temporary one. Concentrate on being practical and enjoying simple pleasures.

August 5th, 14th, 23rd
Guide Numbers: 1, 9, 5

An unexpected event or change in plans could test your ability to adjust and be resourceful. Be adaptable to new situations and take advantage of opportunities that may arise. A romantic encounter may add some intrigue to your day.

Your Daily Numerology

August 6th, 15th, 24th
Guide Numbers: 1, 9, 6

It's not a good time to argue, and you may have to give in on certain things in order to settle a dispute. Strive for harmony in your surroundings and be willing to extend a helping hand when needed.

August 7th, 16th, 25th
Guide Numbers: 1, 9, 7

Although you may be having feelings of uncertainty, have faith that things will work out for the best. Be selective and discriminating, but keep an open mind as well. Opportunities for learning are likely to present themselves now.

August 8th, 17th, 26th
Guide Numbers: 1, 9, 8

Action is the keyword for today. This is a good time to take care of business matters and to get out and accomplish those things you've been planning or thinking about. Be creative and assertive while tending to your responsibilities.

August 9th, 18th, 27th
Guide Numbers: 1, 9, 9

Humanitarian interests highlight your day; something you experience could teach you compassion and humility. Although you may feel as though you are in a stage of transition as you formulate plans for the future, don't dwell on the past.

SEPTEMBER
Guide Numbers: 1, 1

New interests and opportunities are in focus this month; it is a time to act independently. Do not expect others to relieve you of your burdens. Though someone may try to influence your plans, make sure to do things the way you think best. Keep in mind, however, that tact and diplomacy achieve better results than rash headstrong action. A health matter (not necessarily your own) may require attention.

The 1 Year: Planting the Seeds

September 1st, 10th, 19th, 28th
Guide Numbers: 1, 1, 2
    You will have a tendency to be gullible, so think before you act. Consider details carefully and make sure you know what you are getting into, whether it concerns business or a personal relationship.

September 2nd, 11th, 20th, 29th
Guide Numbers: 1, 1, 3
    This is a good day to be seen and heard. Romance is indicated, but you may have to initiate it yourself. Don't be afraid to turn on the charm. Your attention span may be shorter than usual, and you may have trouble concentrating on anything for long periods of time.

September 3rd, 12th, 21st, 30th
Guide Numbers: 1, 1, 4
    Practical matters need to be taken care of and may require more of your time than you are willing to spare. Make sure you are prepared to meet all your commitments and that you are diligent and efficient in everything you do.

September 4th, 13th, 22nd
Guide Numbers: 1, 1, 5
    You may be considering a change in some area of your life—your career, a personal relationship or your home. However, don't do anything impulsive. Something unexpected could be the highlight of your day.

September 5th, 14th, 23rd
Guide Numbers: 1, 1, 6
    Although personal endeavors may be uppermost in your mind, responsibilities to others cannot be overlooked. You may have to adjust your schedule when someone close makes demands on your time.

September 6th, 15th, 24th
Guide Numbers: 1, 1, 7

Your Daily Numerology

Your mental energy is higher than your physical energy, making this a good time for study, meditation, attending a lecture, listening to music or even getting lost in a good book. If you have children they may get on your nerves unless they respect your need for privacy.

September 7th, 16th, 25th
Guide Numbers: 1, 1, 8
Action is the keynote: it is a good time to assert yourself in order to further your plans. If you want a raise or promotion, *ask* for it! You may decide to buy or sell something and could find yourself embarking on a business trip.

September 8th, 17th, 26th
Guide Numbers: 1, 1, 9
Plans may be cancelled or you could find yourself finishing off a project of some kind. Take advantage of any spurts of creativity you may be feeling or they could dissipate.

September 9th, 18th, 27th
Guide Numbers: 1, 1, 1
This is a day for new beginnings. It is a time to take the initiative and stand on your own two feet. Make your own decisions rather than depend on others for advice.

OCTOBER
Guide Numbers: 1, 2
Patience and tact are this month's keynotes to success and happiness. Many little things will require your attention. Petty annoyances and delays could be a source of frustration, as could the seemingly inconsiderate demands of those close to you. Social activities and associations with others are highlighted, and you are likely to make an important new friend or renew an old friendship.

October 1st, 10th, 19th, 28th
Guide Numbers: 1, 2, 3
This is a good day to share with friends or loved ones. Self-expression is favored and you may find yourself spending more

The 1 Year: Planting the Seeds

time than usual on the phone. Avoid being critical or moody. Emotional stress could result.

October 2nd, 11th, 20th, 29th
Guide Numbers: 1, 2, 4

Routine work may be unavoidable today. Even though it lacks excitement, you could nevertheless feel a sense of accomplishment as certain chores get done. Time spent outdoors is likely to provide a pleasant interlude that leaves you feeling refreshed and relaxed.

October 3rd, 12th, 21st, 30th
Guide Numbers: 1, 2, 5

You may find yourself doing something quite different than you had originally planned. Be open to new experiences, but take care lest restlessness and irritability lead to an impulsive remark or action that you could find yourself regretting.

October 4th, 13th, 22nd, 31st
Guide Numbers: 1, 2, 6

Responsibilities cannot be avoided, and some compromise or adjustment will be necessary. However, don't allow yourself to be imposed upon. Remember that you can't please everyone and avoid meddling or giving unwanted advice, or it may backfire, leaving you the injured party.

October 5th, 14th, 23rd
Guide Numbers: 1, 2, 7

Intellectual stimulation is favored: you could learn something new via the media, through reading a book or while conversing with a friend. Try to maintain an optimistic outlook and replace fears with faith that things will work out.

October 6th, 15th, 24th
Guide Numbers: 1, 2, 8

If your expectations of others are unrealistically high, you could be in for a disappointment. Use good judgment and pay attention to little details as well as to those things you consider more significant.

Your Daily Numerology

October 7th, 16th, 25th
Guide Numbers: 1, 2, 9

Interaction with others can be an emotional experience; you are likely to be deeply affected by their words, moods and behavior. Since you're so influenced by your environment, try to seek pleasant surroundings and the company of positive people.

October 8th, 17th, 26th
Guide Numbers: 1, 2, 1

Be prepared for independent action. This is a time to take the initiative and work toward your goals, but try not to come across as too forceful or aggressive. Willingness to meet others half-way achieves better results than being headstrong.

October 9th, 18th, 27th
Guide Numbers: 1, 2, 2

This is a day for sharing with others. Little things may bother you, but try not to overreact. You have more to gain by being patient, tactful and diplomatic. Ask yourself if you're being oversensitive or petty before making a big issue out of a momentary annoyance.

NOVEMBER
Guide Numbers: 1, 3

Creativity and enthusiasm are this month's keynotes to success and happiness, but you must guard against impulsively saying something that you may regret later. Social activities are a source of pleasure and the accent is on friends and romance. You will have more free time now in which to pursue your personal interests. Shopping is favored, but try not to be extravagant.

November 1st, 10th, 19th, 28th
Guide Numbers: 1, 3, 4

Practical matters require your attention, and it is important to face facts and be realistic. Try not to let your emotions interfere with good common sense. Problems can get ironed out faster than you think if you are organized and efficient.

The 1 Year: Planting the Seeds

November 2nd, 11th, 20th, 29th
Guide Numbers: 1, 3, 5
　　Unexpected news or events may cause you to interrupt your normal routine today. Channel your efforts into something creative and avoid being hasty or careless. For those who are unattached, a chance meeting could lead to romance.

November 3rd, 12th, 21st, 30th
Guide Numbers: 1, 3, 6
　　You may have to make some compromise or adjustment because of a friend or loved one. Although you may not be overjoyed at the prospect, it could lead to a glow of satisfaction later on. Try not to force your views or opinions on others.

November 4th, 13th, 22nd
Guide Numbers: 1, 3, 7
　　Mental energy is high, making this a good time to expand your knowledge. Writing is also favored, whether it be catching up on correspondence or jotting down your thoughts in a diary. There could be some confusion surrounding a loved one or friend.

November 5th, 14th, 23rd
Guide Numbers: 1, 3, 8
　　You won't want to be restricted today, whether in spending money or trying out a new idea at work. Someone you meet could help you get something you want—feel free to ask. It's okay to be aggressive now as long as you are not offensive.

November 6th, 15th, 24th
Guide Numbers: 1, 3, 9
　　Self-expression and creative activities are favored, but make sure you speak clearly and choose your words with care so as to avoid any misunderstandings in your communications. It is important to listen carefully as well.

November 7th, 16th, 25th
Guide Numbers: 1, 3, 1
　　Energy and optimism are high, but try not to get carried away by enthusiasm or talk too much about your plans. Careless

words and impulsive actions are likely to be regretted later. A new friend or romantic prospect may enter your life.

November 8th, 17th, 26th
Guide Numbers: 1, 3, 2
    You may find yourself doing a favor for a loved one or friend, or someone could wind up doing one for you. You are likely to be greatly influenced by your environment. Take care not to let yourself be talked into anything you're not sure you want.

November 9th, 18th, 27th
Guide Numbers: 1, 3, 3
    Chance encounters could enrich or complicate your life. Socialize and enjoy yourself, but don't waste time in idle chatter or gossip. Although you may feel like being pampered and appreciated, try not to get upset if things don't work out that way.

DECEMBER
Guide Numbers: 1, 4
    Practicality and economy are called for this month as responsibilities increase and many expenses need to be met. Although contracts look promising, there are still details to be worked out. Firm foundations must be built in all areas of your life, especially where your associations with others are concerned. Try not to lash out at those close to you. Your home is in focus and there could be a change in your living conditions.

December 1st, 10th, 19th, 28th
Guide Numbers: 1, 4, 5
    An unexpected situation could well be a source of tension. People in your environment may be hard to handle, and carelessness could make you accident-prone. Take care not to overlook a practical matter that might require your attention.

December 2nd, 11th, 20th, 29th
Guide Numbers: 1, 4, 6
    Domestic responsibilities require your attention, and you probably won't have as much free time as you would like. A health

The 1 Year: Planting the Seeds

or financial matter should not be neglected, no matter how insignificant it may seem. Sharing a meal with friends or loved ones could be the highlight of your day.

December 3rd, 12th, 21st, 30th
Guide Numbers: 1, 4, 7

You may not be feeling up to par and would benefit from taking some time off by yourself. Quiet pursuits such as gardening or working on a hobby can be uplifting. Don't try to force any issues of a business or financial nature—you could be disappointed with the results.

December 4th, 13th, 22nd, 31st
Guide Numbers: 1, 4, 8

This is a good day to take care of practical matters, whether they pertain to home, finances, career or health. If you stick to your decisions and organize your affairs so you can act the most efficiently, things should start falling into place.

December 5th, 14th, 23rd
Guide Numbers: 1, 4, 9

Something you've been waiting for may come through. On the other hand, you may feel restricted or disappointed in some way. Try not to lash out at those in your environment whose actions displease you.

December 6th, 15th, 24th
Guide Numbers: 1, 4, 1

This is a good day to get started on a new project you have been contemplating for a while. Family duty may seem to interfere with your plans, but you can work around it if you try. Concentrate on what is most important and don't let obstacles stand in your path.

December 7th, 16th, 25th
Guide Numbers: 1, 4, 2

Little things can bring joy or frustration according to your mood. Try not to lose your temper over annoying details or you may lose more than you gain. This is a time for sharing with others, and your patience will be appreciated.

Your Daily Numerology

December 8th, 17th, 26th
Guide Numbers: 1, 4, 3

You'll want to know what's going on, and talking with friends or co-workers may take up a good deal of your time. However, take care not to get into trouble on account of it. Although you may be in a more relaxed frame of mind, try not to lose sight of what needs to be done.

December 9th, 18th, 27th
Guide Numbers: 1, 4, 4

Practical matters need to be taken care of and may require more of your time than you are willing to spare. Although you may feel restricted or disappointed in some way, diligence and self-discipline pay off. However, you should try to avoid being rigid or stubborn.

CHAPTER THREE

THE 2 YEAR

"The Seeds Are Taking Root"

GUIDE NUMBER: 2
COLOR: ORANGE

This is the year to sit back and be patient. Use it to accumulate facts, to renew old friendships, to end quarrels and to pay special attention to the needs of loved ones. Give the seeds planted last year a chance to germinate and mature. Being impatient or trying to force results is as damaging as trying to pull seedlings up by the roots. Delays may seem annoying but are a necessity. Use this time to take care of details rather than to initiate any drastic changes.

This is a year to form friendships or partnerships, to join clubs and to take part in group activities. Be receptive to the ideas of others and be willing to listen to their point of view. Follow their lead and try to emulate their ideas. Whenever possible, avoid making important decisions and try to remain in the background.

You are likely to be feeling more sensitive and touchy than usual, but try not to take everything personally or make mountains out of molehills. Although blue moods may be frequent and tears may lie close to the surface, don't let this emotional vulnerability get you down.

Success and happiness come from being tactful, diplomatic and cooperative in your dealings with others. Avoid being oversensitive, argumentative and petty.

Your Daily Numerology

JANUARY
Guide Numbers: 2, 3

Creativity and self-expression are this month's keynotes to success and happiness, but try not to scatter yourself in too many directions. You are likely to feel an urge to redecorate or pursue some artistic endeavor that has been neglected for a while. Friends and social activities are a source of pleasure, making this a good time to entertain and be entertained.

January 1st, 10th, 19th, 28th
Guide Numbers: 2, 3, 4

This may not be the best day to embark on a new enterprise. Instead, make use of it to attend to routine chores. You can get a lot accomplished if you put your mind to it, but be sure to save some time for a loved one as well.

January 2nd, 11th, 20th, 29th
Guide Numbers: 2, 3, 5

A social gathering is likely to turn out differently than you had anticipated. You stand to benefit from promoting yourself and your ideas. Something unexpected may turn up concerning a child or pet.

January 3rd, 12th, 21st, 30th
Guide Numbers: 2, 3, 6

Someone may need your help or advice. Try to be of service without getting emotionally involved. This is a good time to entertain, and having friends over for dinner could be a source of pleasure.

January 4th, 13th, 22nd, 31st
Guide Numbers: 2, 3, 7

You have more mental energy than physical; time out for rest and relaxation is a must. Writing letters to friends, taking in a show or even curling up with a good book can help to refresh and regenerate you.

January 5th, 14th, 23rd
Guide Numbers: 2, 3, 8

The 2 Year: The Seeds Are Taking Root

Be cordial in your dealings with others—you stand to benefit from the contacts you make. An extravagant urge could lead you to purchase something expensive you don't really need, so exercise good judgment when handling money.

January 6th, 15th, 24th
Guide Numbers: 2, 3, 9
Hurt feelings and misunderstandings could result when those close to you react in ways you find difficult to understand. Try to take minor upsets in your stride without letting your emotions gain the upper hand.

January 7th, 16th, 25th
Guide Numbers: 2, 3, 1
Take time with your appearance. You will feel better about yourself if you know you look your best. A new friend is about to enter your life, and if you're unattached, a chance meeting could lead to romance. However, you may have to make the first move.

January 8th, 17th, 26th
Guide Numbers: 2, 3, 2
This is a good time to do something you enjoy with your mate or friends, but try not to let oversensitivity ruin your day. Words spoken in jest could upset you unless you keep things in their proper perspective.

January 9th, 18th, 27th
Guide Numbers: 2, 3, 3
This is a good day to be seen and heard. Words are likely to flow more freely, and you should have no trouble expressing what's on your mind. Social events are a source of pleasure, and you may impulsively indulge in a shopping spree.

FEBRUARY
Guide Numbers: 2, 4
Practicality and patience are the keynotes to success and happiness this month. There is much work to be done and details require your careful attention. Delays may prove irritating, as

could the numerous household chores that seem almost unending. Be sure to pay attention to your diet.

February 1st, 10th, 19th, 28th
Guide Numbers: 2, 4, 5
   Obligations and commitments keep you busy: you are likely to have many errands to run. A feeling of restriction or frustration could arise when something unexpected gives you yet another responsibility to shoulder.

February 2nd, 11th, 20th, 29th
Guide Numbers: 2, 4, 6
   Write down all the things you have to do, so you won't forget anything. If you have plans to meet someone, be sure you're both clear as to time and place. A friend or loved one may need your special attention.

February 3rd, 12th, 21st
Guide Numbers: 2, 4, 7
   Something in your life could be a source of irritation. Have faith that the situation *will* improve and picture it as you would like it to be. You will need to work diligently, but try to take some time out to rest.

February 4th, 13th, 22nd
Guide Numbers: 2, 4, 8
   You may be offered a promotion or a new assignment in recognition of your past performance. It may not appear to be a giant step forward, but this is a time to advance slowly and surely rather than by leaps and bounds.

February 5th, 14th, 23rd
Guide Numbers: 2, 4, 9
   Loose ends need to be tied up before you can proceed to something new, but don't try to do everything yourself. Be patient with others, even if they seem to be slow, and give them a chance to help.

February 6th, 15th, 24th
Guide Numbers: 2, 4, 1

The 2 Year: The Seeds Are Taking Root

You may find yourself trying something new on a small scale, such as a new way to get to work, a new soap or a new restaurant. Take others into consideration as you go about your personal affairs lest you unwittingly upset someone along the way.

February 7th, 16th, 25th
Guide Numbers: 2, 4, 2

Patience is your greatest asset. Many details need to be taken care of, and you may feel restricted in some way. Try not to let a disappointment discourage you. Friends are more than willing to come to your aid.

February 8th, 17th, 26th
Guide Numbers: 2, 4, 3

It may take courage on your part to bring up something you've been holding inside, but you'll feel much better after it's aired and settled. Treat yourself to something special—a bouquet of flowers for your table, perhaps.

February 9th, 18th, 27th
Guide Numbers: 2, 4, 4

Proceed with your daily affairs in an orderly and systematic fashion. Things may not be moving along as fast as you'd hope, but don't get impatient or testy because of it. Try to keep a sense of humor. This is a time to persevere in spite of obstacles.

MARCH
Guide Numbers: 2, 5

Travel and change are in the air this month as you become exposed to new interests and new contacts. Expect the unexpected. Routine is likely to be broken up by the many activities that take place. Try not to act impulsively, as aggressive behavior or an unwarranted outburst of temper could lead to the rupture of a partnership or association.

March 1st, 10th, 19th, 28th
Guide Numbers: 2, 5, 6

You could be presented with an unexpected new responsibility. A friend may ask you for a commitment that you don't feel quite ready to make. Consider what's best all around before becoming involved.

March 2nd, 11th, 20th, 29th
Guide Numbers: 2, 5, 7
    This is a day to think about your problems quietly rather than broadcast them to anyone who will listen. Although delays or confusion may be particularly frustrating, there is little you can do about it at this time. Trying something new with a close friend could give your spirits a lift.

March 3rd, 12th, 21st, 30th
Guide Numbers: 2, 5, 8
    A feeling of confidence prevails and a pleasant lunch with friends or a productive business meeting could be the highlight of your day. Be flexible to minor changes in your schedule.

March 4th, 13th, 22nd, 31st
Guide Numbers: 2, 5, 9
    Today can bring elation or depression, celebration or regret. It is not a day of status quo. You are likely to wind up sharing a happy occasion with a friend or receiving unpleasant news about someone you know.

March 5th, 14th, 23rd
Guide Numbers: 2, 5, 1
    This is a good day to focus on promoting yourself and your ideas. Your popularity is likely to be high, and you could meet some interesting people. Others are willing to go along with your plans—be appreciative of their support.

March 6th, 15th, 24th
Guide Numbers: 2, 5, 2
    Unexpected aggravations may require all the patience you can muster. Don't let delayed trains, nasty waiters or muddy footprints on your clean floor antagonize you so much that you take it out on the first person to come along.

March 7th, 16th, 25th
Guide Numbers: 2, 5, 3

The 2 Year: The Seeds Are Taking Root

Although this is a social day, it can bring some emotional stress. You may be upset over something you hear or you could wear yourself out by trying to do too much. Plan to work or be with friends—you may tend to brood if you're alone.

March 8th, 17th, 26th
Guide Numbers: 2, 5, 4

You may meet or have some dealings with an older person. An opportunity to increase your financial security that seems like drudgery at first is likely to pay off later on. Put your ideas into practical form.

March 9th, 18th, 27th
Guide Numbers: 2, 5, 5

Your normal routine is likely to be broken—hopefully by something pleasant. It's a good time to be on vacation, to attend a party or to explore some new interest. Try not to let someone else's shortcomings upset you.

APRIL
Guide Numbers: 2, 6

Family responsibilities are highlighted this month. Those close to you place demands on your time, and you are likely to find yourself making several adjustments where your own desires are concerned. A compromise or sacrifice of some sort may be necessary in order to keep peace and harmony in an important relationship.

April 1st, 10th, 19th, 28th
Guide Numbers: 2, 6, 7

You are likely to be feeling very emotional, whether excited about a trip, upset over some news, resentful at being taken for granted, or just plain depressed for no apparent cause. Take time out to be by yourself and think things through.

April 2nd, 11th, 20th, 29th
Guide Numbers: 2, 6, 8

Your Daily Numerology

Don't let someone talk you into something you feel uneasy about. Use good judgment when making any decisions. Trying to be all things to all people is an impossible feat and will not bring the expected results.

April 3rd, 12th, 21st, 30th
Guide Numbers: 2, 6, 9

You may be disappointed over the way a meeting with someone or an event turns out. However, feeling guilty or worrying about it won't accomplish a thing. Keep avenues of communication open and let things take their natural course.

April 4th, 13th, 22nd
Guide Numbers: 2, 6, 1

You may have to take the initiative when a matter requires attention. However, those close to you are willing to help you out and give you moral support. A new responsibility could come your way that may or may not be welcome.

April 5th, 14th, 23rd
Guide Numbers: 2, 6, 2

This is a good day to work with others on a group or community project. You may have to adjust to someone else's idiosyncrasies, and a compromise of some sort could be necessary. Present your ideas but be willing to listen to other viewpoints as well.

April 6th, 15th, 24th
Guide Numbers: 2, 6, 3

This is a good day to plan a party or attend a social gathering. If you have children, this event could center around them. Communications are highlighted, and you may feel like talking and catching up on news.

April 7th, 16th, 25th
Guide Numbers: 2, 6, 4

This is a day to take care of practical matters, especially in the home. You are likely to feel restricted in some way and may resent the many demands made on your time. Try to release some of that pent-up energy through a physical activity you enjoy.

The 2 Year: The Seeds Are Taking Root

April 8th, 17th, 26th
Guide Numbers: 2, 6, 5

A meeting with a friend or loved one may turn out differently than you anticipated. He or she could do anything from embarrassing you in a restaurant to surprising you with a gift. Be adaptable and willing to make adjustments.

April 9th, 18th, 27th
Guide Numbers: 2, 6, 6

Duties and responsibilities to others are highlighted today, but try not to waste valuable energy worrying about domestic, financial or romantic problems you can do nothing about. Being cooperative and kind to those close to you will earn you their appreciation and create harmony in your surroundings.

MAY
Guide Numbers: 2, 7

Emotional sensitivity and lowered vitality could put a damper on your spirits this month. Try to avoid feelings of self-pity and depression. Although the actions of others may upset you, there is little you can do to force issues at this point. You gain more through patience and inner tranquility than by making demands. Take time out to rest.

May 1st, 10th, 19th, 28th
Guide Numbers: 2, 7, 8

You may feel confused about some issue. Seeking advice from someone who's not emotionally involved could help you see things more clearly. Don't be upset if you have to wait for something you want *now*. Headstrong tactics only make matters worse.

May 2nd, 11th, 20th, 29th
Guide Numbers: 2, 7, 9

If you don't have a chance to get out, you could feel confined and a bit sorry for yourself. Counteract these feelings by keeping busy and planning something you can look forward to later. Settle any unfinished business you've been putting aside.

Your Daily Numerology

May 3rd, 12th, 21st, 30th
Guide Numbers: 2, 7, 1
   You may feel like being alone if you're with people and lonely if you're by yourself. Others may have trouble understanding your actions and reactions, and so may you. Discussing a favorite subject with loved ones could be a source of pleasure.

May 4th, 13th, 22nd, 31st
Guide Numbers: 2, 7, 2
   You are likely to be sensitive about little things—a chance remark, a look or glance. Although the actions of others may upset you, there is little you can do to force issues at this time. You gain more through being patient and poised than by making demands. Sit back and relax!

May 5th, 14th, 23rd
Guide Numbers: 2, 7, 3
   You could have an urge to do something creative or impulsively decide to go on a trip or call a friend. Since you won't be content with the same old routine, plan to do something different just for fun.

May 6th, 15th, 24th
Guide Numbers: 2, 7, 4
   Practical matters must be dealt with. Frustrations seem to abound, but you have more to gain at the moment by being patient and tactful than by being stubborn or argumentative.

May 7th, 16th, 25th
Guide Numbers: 2, 7, 5
   Unexpected news, travel or company may come your way. Don't ruin a pleasant time with friends by overindulgence of any kind. You may have trouble doing things in moderation; your will power is likely to be low.

May 8th, 17th, 26th
Guide Numbers: 2, 7, 6
   Something in your day will be emotionally trying, and you may find yourself beset by more aggravation than usual. Try not to insist on having your own way in everything. You are more

The 2 Year: The Seeds Are Taking Root

likely to enjoy the company of loved ones if you are willing to give a little.

May 9th, 18th, 27th
Guide Numbers: 2, 7, 7

A feeling of melancholy could lead you to seek some sort of escape. Rather than brood over an imagined wrong, try talking about what's bothering you. Something that seems minor to others may be important to you, but they won't know unless you tell them so.

JUNE
Guide Numbers: 2, 8

Good judgment and efficiency are this month's keynotes to success and happiness. Take care not to let your emotions rule your head or be influenced by sentimentality. Cooperation is still a must and selfishness in a relationship could lead to a separation. Seek expert advice before making changes. Financial conditions improve through the help of others.

June 1st, 10th, 19th, 28th
Guide Numbers: 2, 8, 9

If you've been working hard, you may receive some form of recognition. Although it is more likely to be a compliment than a raise, don't knock it. You are probably feeling more emotional than usual now. Try to avoid an outburst that could cause hurt feelings.

June 2nd, 11th, 20th, 29th
Guide Numbers: 2, 8, 1

This is a good day to embark on something that could be of benefit to you in your career. It is a time to be assertive and ask for what you want, but that doesn't mean you won't be called upon to compromise or be understanding. Patience and tact in your dealings with others is a must.

June 3rd, 12th, 21st, 30th
Guide Numbers: 2, 8, 2

You will gain by cooperating with others and listening to their opinions. Although you may find little things that have to be worked out annoying, being impatient won't accomplish much and could even set you back. Focus on *results*.

June 4th, 13th, 22nd
Guide Numbers: 2, 8, 3

Friends and social activities are highlighted, and you may feel like organizing a party or a little get-together. Try not to let your emotions rule your head, especially where your finances are concerned. You may have a tendency to be extravagant.

June 5th, 14th, 23rd
Guide Numbers: 2, 8, 4

You may feel burdened today by all the work you have to do or by financial limitations. Take things one step at a time and don't get flustered. Others are in the same boat; you can find comfort in sharing with them.

June 6th, 15th, 24th
Guide Numbers: 2, 8, 5

A new friendship you make through work could lead to romance later on. In fact, sparks could fly when you least expect them to. If an opportunity comes your way, be sure to realize it as one before it's too late.

June 7th, 16th, 25th
Guide Numbers: 2, 8, 6

A compromise may be necessary in order to keep peace in a relationship. A pleasant meal in harmonious surroundings would be a good place to iron out any difficulties. Don't be afraid to ask others for help if your responsibilities become overwhelming.

June 8th, 17th, 26th
Guide Numbers: 2, 8, 7

This is a good day to study something, read or organize data for a report. If your mind isn't active on some mental project, you could fall into a mood of depression or self-pity. Set goals and work toward them.

The 2 Year: The Seeds Are Taking Root

June 9th, 18th, 27th
Guide Numbers: 2, 8, 8
Money is likely to be on your mind, and you may want to get some advice from an expert concerning your finances. Try not to let your emotions interfere with good judgment when it comes to making decisions.

JULY
Guide Numbers: 2, 9
Let go of any activity or relationship that no longer seems to be an important part of your life. Separation from a loved one is possible now and emotional turmoil is likely unless you avoid dwelling on the past. Avoid being oversensitive, petty or jealous. Tying up loose ends leaves more time for pleasure and gives you the freedom to look to the future and proceed on your own.

July 1st, 10th, 19th, 28th
Guide Numbers: 2, 9, 1
You may feel like taking off on your own, but that doesn't mean you won't be called upon to compromise or make adjustments. Someone may need your shoulder to lean on and would appreciate your kindness and understanding.

July 2nd, 11th, 20th, 29th
Guide Numbers: 2, 9, 2
You are likely to be feeling oversensitive; little things may bother you more than they should. Try to look on the bright side of things and share an activity with someone close.

July 3rd, 12th, 21st, 30th
Guide Numbers: 2, 9, 3
Find some time to do something you enjoy. Social activities are highlighted—you could make a new friend. Your thoughts are likely to be engaged in flights of fantasy, making it hard for you to concentrate on anything for very long.

July 4th, 13th, 22nd, 31st
Guide Numbers: 2, 9, 4

Your Daily Numerology

    Reality is likely to rear its head in even the most idyllic of circumstances. Little things will come up that have to be dealt with and practical decisions will need to be made. Try not to lose your temper with someone close to you.

July 5th, 14th, 23rd
Guide Numbers: 2, 9, 5
    You may be torn in so many directions that you could easily wear yourself out if you try to do too much. Don't let an unexpected delay upset you, even though it puts a damper on a certain situation. More than likely it will be only temporary.

July 6th, 15th, 24th
Guide Numbers: 2, 9, 6
    The emphasis is on domestic concerns; you could find yourself drawn into an argument. Try not to get overly emotional. Disputes should be settled in a calm and logical way.

July 7th, 16th, 25th
Guide Numbers: 2, 9, 7
    This is a day to be slow and deliberate. Hasty actions may be regretted later. Try to find a positive outlet for your nervous energy and handle life's problems with objectivity. Listening to music or reading something inspirational could give you a lift.

July 8th, 17th, 26th
Guide Numbers: 2, 9, 8
    Good judgment is needed in *all* your dealings—especially where making decisions is concerned. Don't let your emotions rule your head. A remark by a friend or co-worker may annoy you, but you would be wise to count to ten before giving vent to an outburst of temper.

July 9th, 18th, 27th
Guide Numbers: 2, 9, 9
    This is likely to be an emotional day. Your feelings are easily hurt and you may be disappointed by the actions of those close to you. Conclusions are in the air, and you may find yourself finishing off a project or ending a relationship.

The 2 Year: The Seeds Are Taking Root

AUGUST
Guide Numbers: 2, 1

New conditions and ideas turn your attention to the future and a fresh start. Although inaction on the part of others may upset you, try not to let small business or personal annoyances create tension that could affect your health. Be careful what you say. Forcing issues leads to regrets. Those close to you need to be handled with patience and tact.

August 1st, 10th, 19th, 28th
Guide Numbers: 2, 1, 2

You may find yourself working on a project that seems like it will never end, but patience is a must. This is not a good time to rush. Skimming over something that requires careful consideration could result in your overlooking an important detail.

August 2nd, 11th, 20th, 29th
Guide Numbers: 2, 1, 3

Do something you enjoy with your mate or friends today. You can get a great deal of satisfaction from relationships. If you use your energy to be creative and please others, you won't be sorry you did.

August 3rd, 12th, 21st, 30th
Guide Numbers: 2, 1, 4

The day may seem a bit slow moving; if you have a job you may feel that quitting time will never arrive. A malfunctioning car, appliance or elevator could add to your frustrations. Work around obstacles rather than let them bring you to a halt.

August 4th, 13th, 22nd, 31st
Guide Numbers: 2, 1, 5

Quick thinking will be a great asset, as you'll most likely have to solve some problem fast. An emotional reaction may be triggered by something unexpected, and you could feel anything from upset over a misunderstanding to excitement about traveling.

August 5th, 14th, 23rd
Guide Numbers: 2, 1, 6

Your Daily Numerology

You are likely to find yourself in a situation where you will want your own way. Be prepared, however, to compromise. A warm heart and a helping hand will get you further than argument.

August 6th, 15th, 24th
Guide Numbers: 2, 1, 7

Mental pursuits are favored: you may have flashes of inspiration and intuition. Try to be by yourself for a while so you can rest and contemplate. You could meet someone you've heard a lot about and finally be able to associate a face with that person.

August 7th, 16th, 25th
Guide Numbers: 2, 1, 8

This is a good day to pay your bills or take care of any financial matters. Don't let your emotions interfere with good judgment in personal or business affairs. Lashing out in anger at someone whose actions annoy you is likely to be a cause of regret later.

August 8th, 17th, 26th
Guide Numbers: 2, 1, 9

You may be intent on finishing something old so that you can go on to something new. Romance is also highlighted, and you could be excited about seeing someone who has been away for a while.

August 9th, 18th, 27th
Guide Numbers: 2, 1, 1

This is a good day to start a new project. It is a time to be independent and forge ahead on your own. Your energy level is high—you should be able to accomplish a great deal.

SEPTEMBER
Guide Numbers: 2, 2

Friends and loved ones play an important part this month. Be sociable and join in group activities. Although you may feel that others have overlooked your interests, patience and cooperation are important. Don't let small things upset your peace of mind.

The 2 Year: The Seeds Are Taking Root

September 1st, 10th, 19th, 28th
Guide Numbers: 2, 2, 3
 You are likely to be influenced by your environment: pessimistic people will depress you; jovial types will put you in a good mood. It is a good time to enjoy friends and creative activities, but be selective about the company you keep.

September 2nd, 11th, 20th, 29th
Guide Numbers: 2, 2, 4
 Petty annoyances may be a source of frustration, and you are likely to feel limited in some way. Although there is a need to be practical and efficient, try not to undertake more than is wise. Others are willing to help if you ask them to.

September 3rd, 12th, 21st, 30th
Guide Numbers: 2, 2, 5
 Something unexpected could change your plans or upset your routine. Although you may be annoyed at first, things will probably turn out for the best. A love interest could put you in a sentimental mood.

September 4th, 13th, 22nd
Guide Numbers: 2, 2, 6
 Today's focus is on your home and loved ones; helping a friend or family member celebrate a special occasion could be highlighted. Don't get discouraged if you fail to see immediate results from your efforts or if you seem unappreciated.

September 5th, 14th, 23rd
Guide Numbers: 2, 2, 7
 You may have hunches about people or situations that turn out to be uncannily accurate. Trust your intuition. Don't let personal problems interfere with your concentration; pay attention to detail.

September 6th, 15th, 24th
Guide Numbers: 2, 2, 8
 This is a good day to organize your affairs and take care of financial matters. Get advice from someone you trust before mak-

ing an important decision. A step that improves your status may seem small now but could prove significant in the future.

September 7th, 16th, 25th
Guide Numbers: 2, 2, 9

You'll probably find yourself making concessions to accommodate friends and associates. As long as you don't feel unfairly taken advantage of, be cooperative and compassionate. Those who need you will appreciate your generosity and understanding.

September 8th, 17th, 26th
Guide Numbers: 2, 2, 1

Something new may be highlighted, from making a new friend to starting a new project at work. Taking the initiative can have favorable results provided you are willing to share and cooperate with others as well. Have patience if something does not move as fast as you hoped.

September 9th, 18th, 27th
Guide Numbers: 2, 2, 2

Your patience is likely to be tested in some way. You may be bothered by things that wouldn't ordinarily do so. Companionship is important; feelings of loneliness and self-pity could result if you have to spend too much time by yourself. Make an effort to be with people—preferably those you love.

OCTOBER
Guide Numbers: 2, 3

Social activities will take up much of your time this month, but take care not to scatter your energies in too many directions. New ideas may start you thinking about the future and have an influence on your plans. Self-expression and self-improvement are highlighted now; any attempts to better yourself will be favorable.

October 1st, 10th, 19th, 28th
Guide Numbers: 2, 3, 4

If you have been extravagant lately, you are likely to feel it now. Practical issues have to be faced and may suddenly bring you down to earth. Something may not work out as planned, and

The 2 Year: The Seeds Are Taking Root

there could be some obstacle or disappointment where a friendship is concerned.

October 2nd, 11th, 20th, 29th
Guide Numbers: 2, 3, 5

This is likely to be an active, social day. Take advantage of opportunities to promote your personal interests, but guard against jumping into something unprepared or being overconfident. An unexpected happening may be remembered for a long time to come.

October 3rd, 12th, 21st, 30th
Guide Numbers: 2, 3, 6

The focus is on relationships. You may find yourself doing a lot of running around and putting the needs of others first. Be willing to do a favor for a friend or loved one, but try not to get emotionally involved.

October 4th, 13th, 22nd, 31st
Guide Numbers: 2, 3, 7

Emotional sensitivity and lowered vitality could make this a difficult day—you may find yourself doing something alone that you would prefer to be doing with a companion, or you could feel frustrated and confused by the actions of others.

October 5th, 14th, 23rd
Guide Numbers: 2, 3, 8

Who you know may be more important than what you know. Contacts can help you in both career and personal life, and you may find yourself combining business and pleasure. Efficiency and good judgment pay off.

October 6th, 15th, 24th
Guide Numbers: 2, 3, 9

Annoying people in your environment may grate on your nerves. Try to handle difficult situations with tact and discretion. A warm heart is likely to get you further than a sharp tongue.

October 7th, 16th, 25th
Guide Numbers: 2, 3, 1

Lectures, lunches or meetings may be highlighted. Do what you can to improve your appearance. You will feel better about yourself if you know you look good.

October 8th, 17th, 26th
Guide Numbers: 2, 3, 2
Be patient and willing to wait, but don't let the world go by without you. Companionship is important and sharing in the happiness of loved ones can be an uplifting experience.

October 9th, 18th, 27th
Guide Numbers: 2, 3, 3
This is likely to be a busy day, so take care not to scatter yourself in too many directions. Be discriminating in your choice of activities and channel your energies into those that are most worthwhile. Creativity is favored.

NOVEMBER
Guide Numbers: 2, 4
Practicality and economy are called for this month. Application to the many tasks at hand is of prime importance, no matter how hemmed in or resentful your many responsibilities may make you feel. Although delays and obstacles can be frustrating, this is not the time to rush anything or to look for short cuts. Think things through carefully and don't neglect important details.

November 1st, 10th, 19th, 28th
Guide Numbers: 2, 4, 5
Something unexpected may interrupt your schedule today and create a mood of excitement or confusion. However, practical matters still require your attention; you will not be able to escape the rigors of daily routine altogether.

November 2nd, 11th, 20th, 29th
Guide Numbers: 2, 4, 6
You are likely to find yourself putting the needs of others first. Domestic responsibilities may keep you busy, and someone close could be counting on you for support. A pleasant social ac-

The 2 Year: The Seeds Are Taking Root

tivity involving family or close friends may be the highlight of the day.

November 3rd, 12th, 21st, 30th
Guide Numbers: 2, 4, 7

Although the actions of others may upset you, there is little you can do to force issues at this time. You gain more through patience and inner poise than by making demands. Handle irritations objectively and try to maintain a sense of humor.

November 4th, 13th, 22nd
Guide Numbers: 2, 4, 8

You may feel frustrated by certain obstacles in your path and find yourself unable to work things out the way you would like. Nevertheless, it is important to use good judgment and keep a clear head. Although this is not a good time to make major decisions, you could plan something on a small scale.

November 5th, 14th, 23rd
Guide Numbers: 2, 4, 9

Try to see things from a broader perspective. Although stressful conflicts may be hard to avoid, you will gain by being tolerant of the opinions of others and keeping your mind open to differing points of view.

November 6th, 15th, 24th
Guide Numbers: 2, 4, 1

You are likely to start something new at work or in the home. Even though you may not be pleased with the way things go at first, give them a chance—you could feel differently later on.

November 7th, 16th, 25th
Guide Numbers: 2, 4, 2

Little things need to be taken care of, and you may feel limited or restricted in some way. Patience is your greatest asset. Try not to let a disappointment get you down. Friends are willing to help you out if you give them a chance.

November 8th, 17th, 26th
Guide Numbers: 2, 4, 3

Friends and social activities are highlighted, and you may be excited about a trip or an evening's entertainment. Use some of your energy to be creative and please others. A chance remark could take you off guard.

November 9th, 18th, 27th
Guide Numbers: 2, 4, 4
Practical matters must be dealt with, and you may find yourself feeling frustrated and hemmed in as chores and aggravations mount. Don't expect too much from others. This is not a good time to trust to luck or chance.

DECEMBER
Guide Numbers: 2, 5
Unexpected occurrences make this an active, eventful month. However, try not to be careless as you rush around or an accident could result. New contacts are highlighted and plans are subject to sudden change. Keeping your cool in the face of an annoying situation can prevent an argument you may regret later.

December 1st, 10th, 19th, 28th
Guide Numbers: 2, 5, 6
You may have a hard time saying "no" and wind up with an added responsibility you probably won't relish. Consider it a challenge and get it over with, rather than complain about it or let it drag on.

December 2nd, 11th, 20th, 29th
Guide Numbers: 2, 5, 7
It is important to be precise in the things you do and say so as to avoid confusion. Try not to let yourself be distracted. Obstacles could appear out of nowhere to trip you up. Keeping your mind on the task at hand can help avoid a careless mistake.

December 3rd, 12th, 21st, 30th
Guide Numbers: 2, 5, 8

The 2 Year: The Seeds Are Taking Root

Don't allow yourself to be ruled by emotion or foolish sentiment. Be efficient and organized in all you do and try to avoid jumping to conclusions or making false accusations. Keep your cool in the face of an annoying situation.

December 4th, 13th, 22nd, 31st
Guide Numbers: 2, 5, 9
   You may feel as though your life is a soap opera and wish you could get away from it all. You could also receive some unpleasant news. A short trip, a walk or seeking the counsel of another may help alleviate some of the emotional turmoil.

December 5th, 14th, 23rd
Guide Numbers: 2, 5, 1
   New ideas, contacts and activities are highlighted and there could be a surprise turn to some event. Try to avoid rash words or actions. You are full of restless energy, making it even more important that you exercise good judgment.

December 6th, 15th, 24th
Guide Numbers: 2, 5, 2
   Little annoyances are likely to test your patience, but try not to let them spoil a potentially happy get-together. An understanding friend could help make you feel better; a romantic interest could help you forget.

December 7th, 16th, 25th
Guide Numbers: 2, 5, 3
   Love and friendship are highlighted, although there could be some emotional stress. This is a good time to promote yourself and your ideas. Someone you meet could be helpful to you later.

December 8th, 17th, 26th
Guide Numbers: 2, 5, 4
   An older person may need to be handled with patience and tact. Try to avoid aggressive behavior or an unwarranted outburst of temper. You may be presented with a good opportunity, but be prepared for hard work and red tape.

Your Daily Numerology

December 9th, 18th, 27th
Guide Numbers: 2, 5, 5

Expect the unexpected: it may be a sudden change in plans or some surprising news. Your daily routine is bound to be disrupted by the many activities that take place. Try not to spread yourself too thin or overlook some important detail.

CHAPTER FOUR

THE 3 YEAR

"First Sprouts Start to Appear"

GUIDE NUMBER: 3
COLOR: YELLOW

This is a social, healthy, romance-prone year. However, it can bring stress unless you gain control over your emotions and avoid negative thinking, jealousy or blaming others. This is a year to enjoy life and have a good time. Travel, pamper yourself, entertain and let yourself be entertained. Widen your circle of friends. Social contacts you make could be beneficial later on. You are likely to become more interested in your appearance and may be tempted to go on a shopping spree for a new wardrobe.

This is a time to be seen and heard, but you should be careful of what you say lest it be misinterpreted. Don't talk too much to the wrong people. Avoid gossip and taking things at face value. Success and happiness come through creative outlets and self-expression, whether writing, lecturing, acting, singing, dancing, painting or playing an instrument. Avoid overspending (which can lead to financial difficulties in the 4 year) and wasting opportunities by scattering your energies in too many directions at once.

JANUARY
Guide Numbers: 3, 4

Practicality is of prime importance this month. You have much to put in order and concentrate on where your material affairs are concerned. Problems need your full attention, and it is important that you not put off dealing with them. Someone close to you may be a source of emotional stress.

January 1st, 10th, 19th, 28th
Guide Numbers: 3, 4, 5

You may have to deviate from your daily schedule due to some unforeseen circumstance beyond your control. Be adaptable to changes in plan. If you miss the show at one theater, remember there is always a second showing.

January 2nd, 11th, 20th, 29th
Guide Numbers: 3, 4, 6

Try to maintain an optimistic frame of mind when faced with responsibilities you don't want. Whether it's a child who needs special attention, a touchy situation at work or an appliance that breaks down, a sense of humor can do wonders toward getting you through a frustrating day.

January 3rd, 12th, 21st, 30th
Guide Numbers: 3, 4, 7

You could be easily irritated if you don't have enough time by yourself. Demanding people and situations may set your nerves on edge and make it hard for you to concentrate on your work.

January 4th, 13th, 22nd, 31st
Guide Numbers: 3, 4, 8

Good judgment and efficiency pay off, enabling you to get a lot done. This is a favorable time to go shopping for something you need, whether it be groceries, a new suit or an item for your home.

January 5th, 14th, 23rd
Guide Numbers: 3, 4, 9

This is a day to forgive and forget. You may want to react with heated emotions to the actions or words of someone close to

The 3 Year: First Sprouts Start to Appear

you, but a sharp retort will be regretted later. Tie up loose ends in your everyday affairs.

January 6th, 15th, 24th
Guide Numbers: 3, 4, 1

This is a good day to get your home or office in shape. Follow that urge to redecorate or rearrange your files. A new assignment may appear difficult, but you should have more than enough energy to handle the challenge.

January 7th, 16th, 25th
Guide Numbers: 3, 4, 2

Patience is a great asset when you are faced with annoying details or delays. You may feel overwhelmed by the many tasks that need your attention, but friends and co-workers will lend a helping hand. Be sure to show your appreciation.

January 8th, 17th, 26th
Guide Numbers: 3, 4, 3

There are many things on your mind, making you easily distracted. Take care not to go to the supermarket without your wallet, lock yourself out of your car or apartment, or go to pick up your clothes from the cleaners without your receipt. Socializing with co-workers can be fun.

January 9th, 18th, 27th
Guide Numbers: 3, 4, 4

It is important to have self-discipline. Try not to neglect important details and make sure you are on time for all your appointments. A confining situation could be a source of frustration.

FEBRUARY
Guide Numbers: 3, 5

The vibration of change surrounds you this month, and it is a good time to seek a promotion or advance yourself in some way. However, don't expect things to turn out as planned. Surprises abound. Take care lest restlessness or impulsive actions make you accident-prone, and try to avoid careless words which may be regretted later.

Your Daily Numerology

February 1st, 10th, 19th, 28th
Guide Numbers: 3, 5, 6
    This is a good day to go out for dinner with your friends or mate, so long as you are flexible and understanding. Try not to make a big issue out of someone being a few minutes late because he or she got stuck in traffic.

February 2nd, 11th, 20th, 29th
Guide Numbers: 3, 5, 7
    This is a good day to spend time with close friends—playing bridge, watching a ball game or going to a lecture or museum. A party may sound like fun, but unless you know the people well you may find yourself wishing you were somewhere else.

February 3rd, 12th, 21st
Guide Numbers: 3, 5, 8
    It's okay to combine business and pleasure, but flexibility is a must. Unexpected circumstances may cause you to change your plans. Not having enough money to buy something you want could be a source of frustration. Think big, but be realistic too.

February 4th, 13th, 22nd
Guide Numbers: 3, 5, 9
    You are likely to feel more frustrated than usual by restrictions or limitations. Your body may have trouble keeping up with your mind, so try not to push yourself too hard.

February 5th, 14th, 23rd
Guide Numbers: 3, 5, 1
    This is a good day to start a vacation or begin a new adventure or romance. You are likely to feel restless and confined by routine situations and the status quo. Someone new, who will help break the monotony, may enter your life.

February 6th, 15th, 24th
Guide Numbers: 3, 5, 2
    The day could bring unexpected delays and irritations. A date, meeting or class could be postponed, cancelled or rescheduled unexpectedly. Do something you enjoy with a friend or loved one.

The 3 Year: First Sprouts Start to Appear

February 7th, 16th, 25th
Guide Numbers: 3, 5, 3

The emphasis is on words, both written and spoken. You may be surprised to find a letter in your mailbox or wind up being the principal speaker at a meeting. It's a good day to go to a beauty parlor or buy a new outfit.

February 8th, 17th, 26th
Guide Numbers: 3, 5, 4

Try to find creative ways of combining work and fun: arrange to meet a friend while walking the dog or prepare a vegetable potluck soup for dinner with whatever you happen to have in your refrigerator. You may find yourself pleasantly surprised by the results.

February 9th, 18th, 27th
Guide Numbers: 3, 5, 5

Try to find some constructive outlet for your energy, otherwise boredom could lead to an eating binge or restlessness to a mishap of some kind. This is a good day to work or play outdoors or to engage in an active sport.

MARCH
Guide Numbers: 3, 6

Adjustments to the ways of those close to you are called for this month. There are many obligations and duties that need to be taken care of, but you should avoid shouldering more than your share. Try not to interfere in the affairs of others or offer unwanted advice. Entertaining friends is likely to be a source of pleasure.

March 1st, 10th, 19th, 28th
Guide Numbers: 3, 6, 7

This is a day of mixed emotions. You could have a wonderful flirtation with someone new, only to discover later on that he or she is attached; or feel unusually pleased about the special lunch you packed for a child, only to learn later that they left it on the bus. Don't dwell on minor disappointments.

Your Daily Numerology

March 2nd, 11th, 20th, 29th
Guide Numbers: 3, 6, 8

You are apt to feel pressured by commitments at home and at work. Use good judgment when planning your schedule, so that you can get the most done in the time you have.

March 3rd, 12th, 21st, 30th
Guide Numbers: 3, 6, 9

This is likely to be a busy day, with the emphasis on services rendered or received. You could find yourself working on a community project or consulting an attorney for legal advice. Don't let your imagination run wild where an important relationship is concerned.

March 4th, 13th, 22nd, 31st
Guide Numbers: 3, 6, 1

As long as you are alert to the needs of others, you should be able to do pretty much what you like. This is a good time to channel your energies into a project you've been considering for a while.

March 5th, 14th, 23rd
Guide Numbers: 3, 6, 2

Be sensitive to the needs of others, but without taking on more than your share. Companionship is important; you should enjoy some pleasant moments with a lover or friend.

March 6th, 15th, 24th
Guide Numbers: 3, 6, 3

Communications of all kinds are highlighted. You may want to do a dozen things at once, but try to concentrate on one at a time. Scattering your energies in too many directions could be self-defeating.

March 7th, 16th, 25th
Guide Numbers: 3, 6, 4

This is a good day to take care of practical matters such as cleaning the house, organizing your paperwork or taking yourself or a loved one to the doctor. Children may be hard to discipline, but don't let them get on your nerves.

The 3 Year: First Sprouts Start to Appear

March 8th, 17th, 26th
Guide Numbers: 3, 6, 5

Your feelings toward an old romantic flame may be rekindled for a while, but don't count on things working out any better this time around. It's a good day to get out and circulate.

March 9th, 18th, 27th
Guide Numbers: 3, 6, 6

The day is a good one for a family outing or get-together. A meal shared with those you love is likely to be the highlight of the day. Although you may be tempted to dish out some advice along with the mashed potatoes, don't interfere unless you're asked.

APRIL
Guide Numbers: 3, 7

Energy is low this month, so it is important that you take time out to rest. Try to remain calm and unemotional even though the actions of others may seem hard to understand. Attempts to force issues will only produce disappointing results. Make sure you read the fine print before signing anything.

April 1st, 10th, 19th, 28th
Guide Numbers: 3, 7, 8

This is a day for constructive efforts. Try not to let sentiment interfere with good judgment. Business matters and material affairs take up much of your time, but you can combine them with pleasure when you have lunch with a client or co-worker.

April 2nd, 11th, 20th, 29th
Guide Numbers: 3, 7, 9

Use your intuition and trust your first impressions. Although you may feel unsure about some issue, you know the answer deep down inside and needn't ask others what they think.

April 3rd, 12th, 21st, 30th
Guide Numbers: 3, 7, 1

Although you may have plans in mind, it's best to proceed slowly and carefully. If you act too forcefully or egotistically, you

Your Daily Numerology

are likely to meet with obstacles and delays and wind up disappointed with the results. Try not to bite off more than you can chew.

April 4th, 13th, 22nd
Guide Numbers: 3, 7, 2

This is a good day to go over details and to scrutinize and perfect your projects. You will be able to catch those little things that ordinarily go unnoticed. Cooperate and share with others—a friend may need your sympathetic ear.

April 5th, 14th, 23rd
Guide Numbers: 3, 7, 3

All forms of communication are highlighted. You may be excited about a special letter or call you receive or a party you've been invited to attend. Being in the right place at the right time could result in a lucky break.

April 6th, 15th, 24th
Guide Numbers: 3, 7, 4

Self-discipline is a must as you deal with mundane chores and boring facts, and it is a good idea to balance your day with some social activity. Getting together with friends at someone's home will give your spirits a lift.

April 7th, 16th, 25th
Guide Numbers: 3, 7, 5

Something unexpected could be highlighted today: perhaps a surprise visitor or winning a prize in a contest. Be adaptable to new opportunities and associates, but be selective and discriminating when faced with a choice.

April 8th, 17th, 26th
Guide Numbers: 3, 7, 6

Although you may feel that domestic problems are interfering with your personal needs, try to take little annoyances in stride. Get what you can done, but save some time for socializing.

April 9th, 18th, 27th
Guide Numbers: 3, 7, 7

The 3 Year: First Sprouts Start to Appear

Your ability to concentrate is high, making this a good time for mental pursuits. Do something to stimulate your mind: write a speech or letter, do research, play a game that requires brainwork or just curl up with a good book.

MAY
Guide Numbers: 3, 8

Material matters are highlighted this month; a business-like attitude is a must. Good judgment and efficiency are the keynotes to success and happiness. Try not to let your emotions rule your head, especially where your finances are concerned. Expenses are likely to be high and careless spending could be regretted later on.

May 1st, 10th, 19th, 28th
Guide Numbers: 3, 8, 9

Make use of all your contacts when bringing some issue to fulfillment. Be decisive and confident and willing to put in long hours to get what you want done. Someone you are unaware of may catch a glimpse of you at an event you both attend.

May 2nd, 11th, 20th, 29th
Guide Numbers: 3, 8, 1

This is a good day for putting your ideas across. You are able to express yourself clearly and convince others to support your cause. A business proposal or invitation that sounds appealing may come your way.

May 3rd, 12th, 21st, 30th
Guide Numbers: 3, 8, 2

It is to your advantage to work and share with others. Be willing to listen to someone else's ideas and opinions. Ways of improving your financial condition may be on your mind, but remember to use good judgment in all business dealings.

May 4th, 13th, 22nd, 31st
Guide Numbers: 3, 8, 3

Your Daily Numerology

You may gain from social contacts today. A friend may be instrumental in your getting a job, or a co-worker could put you in touch with someone who will buy your grandmother's antique hobby horse. Keep your eyes and ears open so you don't miss out on an opportunity.

May 5th, 14th, 23rd
Guide Numbers: 3, 8, 4

Practical matters must be dealt with; it is important to remain diligent and efficient at all times. Although there may be an obstacle in your path, it can be overcome with persistence, determination and a positive attitude.

May 6th, 15th, 24th
Guide Numbers: 3, 8, 5

Your personal freedom is likely to become an issue. Someone looking over your shoulder could make you feel resentful, restricted and confined. Take care lest hasty words create problems between you and a friend or associate. You may receive a surprise gift from an admirer or hear about a new business opportunity.

May 7th, 16th, 25th
Guide Numbers: 3, 8, 6

An experience you had some time ago may be of benefit when it helps prevent you from repeating the same mistake. Doing something nice for a loved one can give your feelings a lift. Why not surprise him or her with a helping hand or a small token of affection.

May 8th, 17th, 26th
Guide Numbers: 3, 8, 7

Domestic, financial or romantic problems will be on your mind, but don't let a confused emotional state interfere with your practical or business transactions. Make sure you look both ways before crossing the street, lock the door when you leave your house and pay attention when counting your change.

May 9th, 18th, 27th
Guide Numbers: 3, 8, 8

The 3 Year: First Sprouts Start to Appear

Who you know may be more important than *what* you know when it comes to getting ahead. However, take care to avoid rash words or actions that could divert opportunity somewhere else. An optimistic attitude coupled with good common sense is your best asset.

JUNE
Guide Numbers: 3, 9

Expand your interests and try to see things from a broader point of view. Matters that require understanding and compassion come to a head. Letting go of a situation or relationship that has outlived its usefulness may seem difficult but will lead to a feeling of release and an improved emotional outlook.

June 1st, 10th, 19th, 28th
Guide Numbers: 3, 9, 1

You may have mixed emotions about some person or situation. Ask yourself if it is making you happier, wiser, more secure or can benefit you in any other way. If the answer is "no," think twice before channelling your time and energy in that direction.

June 2nd, 11th, 20th, 29th
Guide Numbers: 3, 9, 2

Sharing an activity with someone you love is highlighted. Pay attention to little things and show consideration for the feelings of others. You have much to gain by being patient and tactful.

June 3rd, 12th, 21st, 30th
Guide Numbers: 3, 9, 3

Creative endeavors and social activities are likely to be a success, but watch what you say and how you say it. Self-expression is highlighted; words can be your best friend or your worst enemy.

June 4th, 13th, 22nd
Guide Numbers: 3, 9, 4

Practical matters require your attention; money may be an issue. Make sure you are getting the best deal possible before signing any papers. A friend or loved one may cause an emotional upset.

June 5th, 14th, 23rd
Guide Numbers: 3, 9, 5

This is not a day to stay home. Get out and mingle. Your magnetism is high, making this a good time to sell others on your ideas. You may receive some unexpected news about a friend or loved one.

June 6th, 15th, 24th
Guide Numbers: 3, 9, 6

Try to channel your energy into something creative, rather than into arguing or getting too involved in the affairs of others. An outing with loved ones may be a source of pleasure.

June 7th, 16th, 25th
Guide Numbers: 3, 9, 7

This is a good day to get lost in a novel, pretend you're the hero or heroine in a movie, or better yet, write some fiction of your own. Fantasy is good for you as long as you don't overdo it.

June 8th, 17th, 26th
Guide Numbers: 3, 9, 8

This is likely to be an active and productive day, but you should be realistic in your expectations. Use good judgment and efficiency in handling your affairs and be sure to take care and not hurry through something that requires more attention.

June 9th, 18th, 27th
Guide Numbers: 3, 9, 9

You are likely to drift into thoughts of adventure or romance and may have trouble concentrating for any length of time. You could attend a farewell party for a friend who is moving away or even be the one embarking on a trip yourself.

JULY
Guide Numbers: 3, 1

The 3 Year: First Sprouts Start to Appear

Creative, original ideas meet with success this month, as do attempts at self-improvement, redecorating and making new friends. An important decision needs to be faced, and you may feel the urge to start something new. Flirtatious encounters can be fun, but beware of getting involved if one of you is attached. Seek release for pent-up feelings through some constructive outlet.

July 1st, 10th, 19th, 28th
Guide Numbers: 3, 1, 2
Sharing in others' happiness is good for you, but be careful not to let yourself get talked into the wrong thing. You may find yourself involved in a situation that you'll be eager to get out of later. If possible, take time out to enjoy music or art.

July 2nd, 11th, 20th, 29th
Guide Numbers: 3, 1, 3
You may have a creative surge of energy, but take care not to scatter it in too many directions. It's a good time to start doing something to improve your appearance: a new hairstyle or outfit could give you a lift.

July 3rd, 12th, 21st, 30th
Guide Numbers: 3, 1, 4
Something you've refused to accept may come to the fore so strongly that you can no longer delude yourself that it doesn't exist. Face problems logically and practically, rather than by sweeping them under the rug.

July 4th, 13th, 22nd, 31st
Guide Numbers: 3, 1, 5
Something unexpected will be highlighted. If you are unattached, a new romantic prospect with a background quite different from your own may enter your life. If you have a partner, the two of you could be embarking on a trip or adventure of some kind.

July 5th, 14th, 23rd
Guide Numbers: 3, 1, 6

Your Daily Numerology

Loved ones will need your sympathy and understanding, but try not to meddle or give unwanted advice. Interfering in the affairs of others is likely to backfire. Even though you may feel you know what's right, you may stand to gain the most through making a compromise or adjustment.

July 6th, 15th, 24th
Guide Numbers: 3, 1, 7

This is a good day for reading or becoming involved in something of an uplifting nature. Small talk is likely to irritate and bore you, and unless you can share the company of people whose interests are similar to your own, you would be better off being by yourself.

July 7th, 16th, 25th
Guide Numbers: 3, 1, 8

You are likely to have a stroke of good luck, but don't let high spirits cloud your thinking or prevent you from using sound judgment. Take the decisions you are faced with seriously—they could be important to your future.

July 8th, 17th, 26th
Guide Numbers: 3, 1, 9

Don't let your emotions run wild. An outburst of temper could lead to the loss of a valuable friendship. This is a good time to drop a bad habit and vow to make a positive new start.

July 9th, 18th, 27th
Guide Numbers: 3, 1, 1

Concentrate on self-improvement: go for a beauty treatment, take a class or join a gym. Someone new may enter your life who could be of importance later, but it will be up to you to initiate the contact.

AUGUST
Guide Numbers: 3, 2

Short trips and comings and goings back and forth abound this month, and you are likely to feel concern over the problems

The 3 Year: First Sprouts Start to Appear

of others. Try not to be petty or overly emotional, even though everyday annoyances can be aggravating. Patience, tact and attention to details are called for. Be willing to accept the support of friends.

August 1st, 10th, 19th, 28th
Guide Numbers: 3, 2, 3

You are likely to be easily distracted today and have trouble concentrating. Friends and social activities are a source of pleasure, but take care not to get yourself into trouble by talking too much at the wrong time.

August 2nd, 11th, 20th, 29th
Guide Numbers: 3, 2, 4

A practical approach to your problems will prevent needless stress and emotional trauma. Be patient and cooperative when dealing with others. You could find some relief from your cares through a friend's companionship.

August 3rd, 12th, 21st, 30th
Guide Numbers: 3, 2, 5

You are unlikely to have time to get bored and could unexpectedly find yourself sharing in some festivity. Take care to avoid impulsive words or actions which may be regretted later. Someone new may enter your life or someone old may exit.

August 4th, 13th, 22nd, 31st
Guide Numbers: 3, 2, 6

This is a day to be conscientious about meeting your responsibilities. It's a good time to visit someone in the hospital, have a friend over for dinner or tackle tedious chores you've allowed to pile up. Show concern for loved ones, but don't be overprotective.

August 5th, 14th, 23rd
Guide Numbers: 3, 2, 7

Loud noises and congestion may disturb you; you'll probably be better off staying away from crowds. Try not to force any important issues. You have more to gain by being patient and letting things run their course.

August 6th, 15th, 24th
Guide Numbers: 3, 2, 8

Be organized and efficient, but avoid letting oversensitivity gain the upper hand. Although you may not feel that your efforts are appreciated, don't let it get you down. You'll see results later. Deal with emotional upset in a logical, calm manner.

August 7th, 16th, 25th
Guide Numbers: 3, 2, 9

Loose ends get tied up today; some change or completion may come as a relief. You could receive news from or about someone you've been out of touch with for a while. A new friendship may turn into a pleasant romance, but don't count on anything permanent.

August 8th, 17th, 26th
Guide Numbers: 3, 2, 1

You may need to provide someone with a shoulder to lean on. Give advice if asked for, but don't meddle. Romance or travel may be on your mind: you could find yourself initiating an outing with loved ones.

August 9th, 18th, 27th
Guide Numbers: 3, 2, 2

You may be feeling oversensitive and more emotional than usual. Try not to make a big deal out of something that may have been said in jest or let some petty irritation annoy you. Sharing with others can be a source of pleasure.

SEPTEMBER
Guide Numbers: 3, 3

Communications is the keynote to success and happiness this month. However, avoid gossip or unnecessary words. Friends are helpful and may be instrumental in opening new avenues for your personal progress. Your focus is likely to be on how things look. Outer appearance is important, but don't neglect what's inside.

September 1st, 10th, 19th, 28th
Guide Numbers: 3, 3, 4

The 3 Year: First Sprouts Start to Appear

Even though you may be in a frivolous mood, responsibilities must be taken care of; you have a need to be practical. If you organize your time well, you'll be able to accomplish everything you have to and still have time for leisure.

September 2nd, 11th, 20th, 29th
Guide Numbers: 3, 3, 5

Something unexpected may catch you off guard. Act sensibly and don't get overly emotional. Social contacts you make now can be valuable to you later; it's a good idea to accept any invitations that come your way.

September 3rd, 12th, 21st, 30th
Guide Numbers: 3, 3, 6

This is a good day to entertain or be entertained. Friends and family are in focus and you could find yourself making an adjustment to please one of them. Try not to force your views or an emotionally tense situation may result.

September 4th, 13th, 22nd
Guide Numbers: 3, 3, 7

You may experience some confusion or feel annoyed by someone you encounter. Make sure you get your facts straight before jumping to conclusions. Don't let criticism get to you.

September 5th, 14th, 23rd
Guide Numbers: 3, 3, 8

You're in a good cycle for getting ahead through social contacts. Enjoy the day's events, but don't lose sight of common sense. Self-control is important—you should take care not to overreact to things.

September 6th, 15th, 24th
Guide Numbers: 3, 3, 9

You will need an emotional release of some sort—through creative self-expression, travel or sports. Staying home or doing routine work can make you irritable and argumentative.

September 7th, 16th, 25th
Guide Numbers: 3, 3, 1

Today should be relatively obstacle-free; social activities are likely to interest you more than mundane chores. It's a good time to start something new in the way of self-improvement or recreation, like getting a haircut or embarking on a trip.

September 8th, 17th, 26th
Guide Numbers: 3, 3, 2
Some annoyances can be averted by foresight, but others will require patience and common sense. Pettiness could lead to problems in a personal relationship, so try not to make mountains out of molehills.

September 9th, 18th, 27th
Guide Numbers: 3, 3, 3
This is a day to be seen and heard. However, you may be torn in so many directions you could wear yourself out; so don't scatter your energies or be careless. Enjoy the company of friends, but try not to be temperamental or possessive.

OCTOBER
Guide Numbers: 3, 4
Practical matters are highlighted this month; you may feel burdened by responsibilities and details. However, take care to get all your affairs in order, work out any problems at home and stick to a sensible routine. Even though you may have a heavy schedule, your health should not be neglected. Proper diet and some time for rest and relaxation are important too.

October 1st, 10th, 19th, 28th
Guide Numbers: 3, 4, 5
You are unlikely to have time to get bored and may have to adjust your schedule or change your plans. Shopping sprees could bring surprises, and you could wind up with something quite different from what you set out to get.

October 2nd, 11th, 20th, 29th
Guide Numbers: 3, 4, 6

The 3 Year: First Sprouts Start to Appear

You may have to deal with something you don't relish. Those close to you are likely to make demands on your time, and you could feel resentful about some compromise or adjustments you feel forced to make.

October 3rd, 12th, 21st, 30th
Guide Numbers: 3, 4, 7

You are likely to have more mental energy than physical—don't commit yourself to more than you can handle. People may get on your nerves, especially if they're demanding or pry into your personal affairs.

October 4th, 13th, 22nd, 31st
Guide Numbers: 3, 4, 8

Try to avoid indecision or inertia. You can get a lot accomplished if you are efficient and organized. Be sure to exercise good judgment and keep a clear head, even if there is some opposition to your plans.

October 5th, 14th, 23rd
Guide Numbers: 3, 4, 9

You could feel confined by circumstances, but try to look at things from a broader scope and avoid temperamental outbursts. A friend or loved one who annoys you may need your compassion and understanding.

October 6th, 15th, 24th
Guide Numbers: 3, 4, 1

This is a good day to start a home-improvement project or plan an activity that involves family or friends. A loved one could provide emotional support, but there are some things you must do alone.

October 7th, 16th, 25th
Guide Numbers: 3, 4, 2

Sharing can be mutually beneficial to you and those close to you. Tasks that might seem like drudgery if you had to work alone may become much less burdensome if you let others give you a hand. Try not to get bogged down in detail.

Your Daily Numerology

October 8th, 17th, 26th
Guide Numbers: 3, 4, 3

Don't depend on your memory for everything. In your enthusiasm to accept an invitation or try something new, you could overlook a practical matter that needs your attention. You'll have many things to keep track of—it may be wise to make a list.

October 9th, 18th, 27th
Guide Numbers: 3, 4, 4

Practical matters require your attention, and you are likely to feel restricted or disappointed in some way. Strive for balance in your schedule rather than being rigid and unyielding. Some fresh air and exercise could be beneficial.

NOVEMBER
Guide Numbers: 3, 5

Progress is the keynote in this very active month. You are likely to enjoy greater personal freedom and a more public life. Expect the unexpected and be open to opportunities that come your way. This is a good time to meet new people, take up new interests and become involved in new activities. Friends and loved ones are helpful. A trip or a move may be in the offing.

November 1st, 10th, 19th, 28th
Guide Numbers: 3, 5, 6

Domestic issues could interfere with personal plans, giving rise to some frustration. Others seek your help or advice, and although there is much you want to do, adjustments have to be made to the needs of those close to you.

November 2nd, 11th, 20th, 29th
Guide Numbers: 3, 5, 7

There is much for you to consider; you would do well to be selective in your choices. You may be feeling uneasy about something that lies beneath the surface of a situation and yet be unable to pinpoint what it is.

The 3 Year: First Sprouts Start to Appear

November 3rd, 12th, 21st, 30th
Guide Numbers: 3, 5, 8
   Material concerns are highlighted: you should be alert for opportunities to improve your financial status. Someone in a position of authority may be helpful to you. Being in the right place at the right time doesn't hurt either.

November 4th, 13th, 22nd
Guide Numbers: 3, 5, 9
   Restrictions or limitations may prove frustrating. You may feel that you'd like to have more freedom or excitement in your life, but take care not to look for it in the wrong places or ignore the feelings of others while you're pursuing it.

November 5th, 14th, 23rd
Guide Numbers: 3, 5, 1
   New opportunities and experiences come your way: you may find yourself exploring something that never appealed to you before. An idea or inspiration that has been eluding you may pop into your mind, but make sure you jot it down so you won't forget it.

November 6th, 15th, 24th
Guide Numbers: 3, 5, 2
   You may find yourself fussing over details. Little things and unexpected changes in your schedule are likely to irritate you. Don't jump to conclusions where a friend or loved one is concerned. A discouraging situation could change unexpectedly.

November 7th, 16th, 25th
Guide Numbers: 3, 5, 3
   Your social life should be active. Pay special attention to your appearance and to your choice of words. You will probably find yourself doing a lot of talking and may be in the limelight.

November 8th, 17th, 26th
Guide Numbers: 3, 5, 4
   Frustration may result when your plans seem blocked or you feel limited or opposed in some way. However, rather than allow

yourself to get depressed, try to see things from a different point of view. A creative twist could help solve some of your problems.

November 9th, 18th, 27th
Guide Numbers: 3, 5, 5
The focus is on the unexpected: you may be in for a surprise. Take care lest restless energy or a short attention span make you accident prone. Your will power is likely to be low, especialy when it comes to staying on a diet.

DECEMBER
Guide Numbers: 3, 6
Duty and responsibilities are highlighted this month as you become more involved in the affairs of family and friends. Although there is little time for yourself, a feeling of well-being results when you willingly and unselfishly help out someone close to you who seeks your aid. A new love or an emotional matter is a source of pleasure.

December 1st, 10th, 19th, 28th
Guide Numbers: 3, 6, 7
Negative emotions may be hard to avoid when an overcritical person touches a sensitive nerve. You could be feeling irritable and on edge and be affected by something unspoken as much as by anything that is said. Try to avoid making assumptions about a situation.

December 2nd, 11th, 20th, 29th
Guide Numbers: 3, 6, 8
You could be feeling pressured, but try to stay calm and see things in perspective. Listen to what others have to say and consider both sides of a situation before making a decision. Expenses are likely to be high.

December 3rd, 12th, 21st, 30th
Guide Numbers: 3, 6, 9
This could be a day of creative achievements and fulfilled ambitions. However, try not to let your imagination run wild, or a

The 3 Year: First Sprouts Start to Appear

festive or creative mood could be marred by some worry or anxiety. Your magnetism is high and you can easily sway others to your way of thinking.

December 4th, 13th, 22nd, 31st
Guide Numbers: 3, 6, 1
 Something in your life may require a fresh start. If you make sure you know what you want and are willing to face and accept the duties and responsibilities that go along with it, this is a good day to move forward with your plans.

December 5th, 14th, 23rd
Guide Numbers: 3, 6, 2
 Compromise and cooperation are called for. It is a time to make adjustments to the needs of others and to meet your responsibilities with an ungrudging heart. Those close to you will appreciate your thoughtfulness and understanding, and a gentle touch or kiss may mean more to them than words can say.

December 6th, 15th, 24th
Guide Numbers: 3, 6, 3
 Friends and children are highlighted; you could find yourself playing the role of host. You will be concerned with the way things look and may spend money on improving your appearance or beautifying your home.

December 7th, 16th, 25th
Guide Numbers: 3, 6, 4
 Home and family are in focus. Problems may need to be ironed out, and you could feel overwhelmed by the many duties and obligations that face you. A travel-connected setback or delay could be a source of frustration.

December 8th, 17th, 26th
Guide Numbers: 3, 6, 5
 You may be tempted to overindulge and have trouble doing things in moderation. Take care not to scatter your energies in so many directions that you neglect your responsibilities. Events may not turn out as planned, and something unexpected could happen at home.

Your Daily Numerology

December 9th, 18th, 27th
Guide Numbers: 3, 6, 6

Family matters are in focus; you may find yourself putting the needs of loved ones before your own. Try not to interfere in the affairs of others unless you are asked. Being critical or fussy could lead to unnecessary strife.

CHAPTER FIVE

THE 4 YEAR

"Digging and Hoeing"

GUIDE NUMBER: 4
COLORS: GREEN, BROWN

This is a year of hard work, structure and limitations. It's a time to put your nose to the grindstone and build firm foundations for the future in all areas—career and health as well as your personal life. Organize your work habits, stick to schedules, eat sensibly, exercise regularly and cultivate solid relationships. This is not a year for frivolity. You are likely to be feeling more serious and conservative than usual. It's possible you may also feel burdened by your job or financial responsibilities, and this could lead you to become stubborn, pessimistic, irritable, narrow-minded or complain of your aches and pains.

This is a good time to invest in property or real estate and make improvements in business or home. Do whatever needs to be done to ensure growth and security for the future. It's a time to settle down, to solidify what is already in your life, to marry or go back to school or work.

Success and happiness come through self-discipline, being systematic and putting ideas into concrete form. Avoid being lazy and disorganized or neglecting your health. You could have some difficulty with your teeth or bones.

Your Daily Numerology

JANUARY
Guide Numbers: 4, 5

You are prone to mood swings and confusion as you feel both the vibration for stability and the vibration for change. Decisions concerning your future should be considered carefully. Nerves may become frayed as you try to free yourself from an undesirable situation. If you're planning a trip, this is a good time to go.

January 1st, 10th, 19th, 28th
Guide Numbers: 4, 5, 6

This is a good day for a family outing or get-together. You may find yourself spending more time than usual in the kitchen, but take some time out to relax as well. If others offer to do the dishes, let them.

January 2nd, 11th, 20th, 29th
Guide Numbers: 4, 5, 7

Psychological insights abound: you would do well to trust your intuition. A quiet evening spent with a close friend or loved one is likely to be a source of pleasure.

January 3rd, 12th, 21st, 30th
Guide Numbers: 4, 5, 8

Your energy level is high and you should be able to get a lot accomplished. Go on a short business trip or take a client out to lunch. Financial matters may be on your mind, but don't neglect the emotional needs of loved ones because of them.

January 4th, 13th, 22nd, 31st
Guide Numbers: 4, 5, 9

You are likely to feel restless and confined unless you keep yourself busy at something you enjoy. Sports may provide a healthy outlet, as could planning to do something out of the ordinary.

January 5th, 14th, 23rd
Guide Numbers: 4, 5, 1

An opportunity that sounds appealing may come your way, but before you jump at it, ask yourself if it offers stability and

The 4 Year: Digging and Hoeing

what the future prospects really are. Avoid being negligent or impractical.

January 6th, 15th, 24th
Guide Numbers: 4, 5, 2

Unexpected details crop up that need to be taken care of without delay. Although it may be hard for you to keep your temper in check, an angry outburst would not be wise. If you deal with the public in any way make sure you are tactful and diplomatic.

January 7th, 16th, 25th
Guide Numbers: 4, 5, 3

You'll enjoy flirting and being noticed. This is a good time to have some fun. Plan some entertainment or an evening with friends. A new person may come into your life in an unexpected way.

January 8th, 17th, 26th
Guide Numbers: 4, 5, 4

You are likely to be in for some hard work, and there may be some obstacle to overcome. Make sure your home and work areas are in order or you could be frustrated by the disarray.

January 9th, 18th, 27th
Guide Numbers: 4, 5, 5

This is a good day to visit with friends, but make sure you keep your schedule flexible. Something unexpected could come up that could cause you to rearrange your plans.

FEBRUARY
Guide Numbers: 4, 6

Family affairs need to be taken care of this month, and you are likely to feel burdened by the demands of those close to you. It may be difficult to find much time for yourself as responsibilities and chores pile up. Resentment could lead to heated words that only aggravate the situation. Be sure not to neglect health or financial issues—no matter how insignificant they may seem.

Your Daily Numerology

February 1st, 10th, 19th, 28th
Guide Numbers: 4, 6, 7

If you can't be with people whose company you enjoy, you'll be better off spending time alone. Others may irritate and annoy you. This is a good day to attend a class on something that could be of benefit to your job.

February 2nd, 11th, 20th, 29th
Guide Numbers: 4, 6, 8

This is a day for doing things that will help improve your home, health or working conditions. It's a good time for a job interview, a visit to the dentist or even reorganizing your closets or files.

February 3rd, 12th, 21st
Guide Numbers: 4, 6, 9

This is a day of mixed emotions; an important relationship could blossom or end, depending on its substance. You may see or hear from someone you've been out of touch with for awhile.

February 4th, 13th, 22nd
Guide Numbers: 4, 6, 1

Take care of all your mundane chores: make enough spaghetti sauce for the week, glue your broken vase back together again, polish your shoes. Someone may need your shoulder to lean on, but try not to take on more than your share of the burden.

February 5th, 14th, 23rd
Guide Numbers: 4, 6, 2

Sentimentality and sensitivity run hand in hand today: little things will mean a lot. You are in the mood for sharing both feelings and good times with those you love and may be easily hurt if they don't react in the way you expect.

February 6th, 15th, 24th
Guide Numbers: 4, 6, 3

The focus is likely to be social—it's a good time to express yourself and your ideas. Pleasure could combine with work: you could be sent to an office on an assignment and end up attending a going-away party for one of their employees.

The 4 Year: Digging and Hoeing

February 7th, 16th, 25th
Guide Numbers: 4, 6, 4
 This is a good day to get your hands dirty by tending to practical and domestic matters. Clean your oven, fuss with your plants or varnish that old bureau. If you cook, try mixing the ingredients with your bare hands, just to feel the texture.

February 8th, 17th, 26th
Guide Numbers: 4, 6, 5
 The day is likely to be unpredictable. An appointment may be cancelled, a visitor may show up unannounced or you could receive some surprise news. If you decide to try a new recipe, make sure you have all the ingredients ready before you begin.

February 9th, 18th, 27th
Guide Numbers: 4, 6, 6
 Run errands and do chores. Examine your priorities and make adjustments where necessary. Your job situation may be on your mind; if you're not working, you may want to start.

MARCH
Guide Numbers: 4, 7
 Health should not be neglected this month: time alone for rest and relaxation is a must. Try to have faith and not take irritations and annoyances too seriously. Things could improve if allowed to run their course. Avoid impulsive actions you may find yourself regretting later. Studying a subject that interests you or perfecting a skill can be rewarding.

March 1st, 10th, 19th, 28th
Guide Numbers: 4, 7, 8
 Something under the surface which you are not aware of could cause a situation to have a different outcome than you imagined. Keep plugging at current tasks and don't let yourself dwell on past mistakes.

March 2nd, 11th, 20th, 29th
Guide Numbers: 4, 7, 9

Your Daily Numerology

This is a good day for finishing things: clean out your refrigerator, add the last footnote to your research project or put a final coat of paint on your car. You may find that your chores go faster if you listen to music while you work.

March 3rd, 12th, 21st, 30th
Guide Numbers: 4, 7, 1

Be discriminating about what thoughts you allow your mind to dwell upon and don't let momentary feelings of discouragement put you in a depressed mood. Channel your energies into realistic goals.

March 4th, 13th, 22nd, 31st
Guide Numbers: 4, 7, 2

You probably won't stray much from your daily routine. Keeping busy gives you a sense of accomplishment and a feeling of contentment with the status quo. Work toward a goal that will improve your situation.

March 5th, 14th, 23rd
Guide Numbers: 4, 7, 3

This is a day to enjoy the company of those you love. Romance is in the air: you could luxuriate in anything from a candlelight dinner to sitting on a park bench in the sun with someone close to you.

March 6th, 15th, 24th
Guide Numbers: 4, 7, 4

If you're having a misunderstanding with someone, try a forthright, realistic approach. Get all the facts before taking any action. Even though you may feel pressured to work long hours, it would be wise to get adequate rest.

March 7th, 16th, 25th
Guide Numbers: 4, 7, 5

Something unexpected could happen that leads to momentary upset or elation. It could be anything from half your party guests cancelling out to someone giving you a present. If you come into some extra money, don't spend it foolishly.

The 4 Year: Digging and Hoeing

March 8th, 17th, 26th
Guide Numbers: 4, 7, 6
The day's focus is on responsibility. You may be feeling resentful of some unsatisfactory situation in your life. However, there's no point in brooding. Change negative thoughts into positive ones and go on with the day's business.

March 9th, 18th, 27th
Guide Numbers: 4, 7, 7
Your concentration is high, making this a good time for mental pursuits. Physical energy may be low, so don't push yourself too hard. You would be better off working by yourself, away from distractions and interruptions.

APRIL
Guide Numbers: 4, 8
Good judgment and organization are the keynotes to success this month. Business matters, including a possible promotion and/or real estate deal, are highlighted. Although there could be some opposition to your plans, don't let your emotions rule your head. It's a good idea to seek expert advice before making investments or signing contracts. Take nothing for granted.

April 1st, 10th, 19th, 28th
Guide Numbers: 4, 8, 9
The day could bring an ending of sorts that could range anywhere from changing garages due to poor service to changing doctors because the one you've been going to has just retired. Be realistic in your expectations and try to keep a broad outlook.

April 2nd, 11th, 20th, 29th
Guide Numbers: 4, 8, 1
Avoid indecision and inertia. *Act* on your ideas. Go for that job interview, present that proposal or ask for that raise. This is a good time to initiate something that could be financially rewarding.

Your Daily Numerology

April 3rd, 12th, 21st, 30th
Guide Numbers: 4, 8, 2

    Working together and sharing are the keynotes of the day. Business matters are highlighted; it's a good idea to seek expert advice. Be willing to meet others halfway.

April 4th, 13th, 22nd
Guide Numbers: 4, 8, 3

    You are likely to be in an enterprising mood and may find yourself doing anything from helping a friend scrub down his boat to selling candy at the PTA. If you're single, a new romantic interest could change your outlook on things.

April 5th, 14th, 23rd
Guide Numbers: 4, 8, 4

    Make sure you keep a clear head and manage all your affairs efficiently. Don't take anything for granted or leave matters to chance. Money could be an issue, but if you have used good judgment all along, your worries about it could be unfounded.

April 6th, 15th, 24th
Guide Numbers: 4, 8, 5

    Be prepared for something unexpected to happen. You could get a haircut that doesn't turn out the way you envisioned. You could go window shopping and wind up with a bargain you just couldn't resist. Take minor upsets in stride and be adaptable to new opportunities that arise.

April 7th, 16th, 25th
Guide Numbers: 4, 8, 6

    You may feel as though you're being asked to do too much when it comes to chores. Try delegating some of your responsibilities to others and eliminating any superfluous tasks. A club or community activity could be highlighted.

April 8th, 17th, 26th
Guide Numbers: 4, 8, 7

    A trip to a quiet place may be just what you need to help resolve some inner struggle. Organize your daily affairs so that you'll have sufficient time to relax.

The 4 Year: Digging and Hoeing

April 9th, 18th, 27th
Guide Numbers: 4, 8, 8

Force yourself to do those tasks you've been putting off for a while. Your efficiency and self-discipline are high and you can get a lot done. Be tolerant of others who operate at a slower pace than you.

MAY
Guide Numbers: 4, 9

It is important that you keep an open mind this month. Try to be tolerant of the opinions of others and listen politely to differing points of view. Take care of your obligations, get rid of anything unproductive in your life and tie up loose ends to clear the way for the new to come in.

May 1st, 10th, 19th, 28th
Guide Numbers: 4, 9, 1

You may feel like doing something just for yourself and won't particularly care if others disagree. However, take care not to forget a commitment or run roughshod over someone close to you. A small favor done now will be appreciated more than you know.

May 2nd, 11th, 20th, 29th
Guide Numbers: 4, 9, 2

Your sensitivity is heightened; this is likely to be an emotional day. Tears may be as easily triggered by a thoughtful gesture or a beautiful sunset as by something someone says. There's lots of work to be done. Let others pitch in and give you a hand.

May 3rd, 12th, 21st, 30th
Guide Numbers: 4, 9, 3

You may have a visit from someone you haven't seen for a while or receive news from far away. Try not to get upset by the criticism of others. Their comments are prompted by their own problems and not by anything you've said or done.

Your Daily Numerology

May 4th, 13th, 22nd, 31st
Guide Numbers: 4, 9, 4

You may have to do something you don't really relish. Although you wish you could be off on a trip somewhere, it just isn't the right time. You can celebrate at a later date, after you've taken care of your responsibilities.

May 5th, 14th, 23rd
Guide Numbers: 4, 9, 5

Events are likely to have a twist of the unexpected, especially where your personal relationships are concerned. You may be disappointed by the behavior of someone you thought you knew well, or you may go out with someone new and be surprised at how the evening ends.

May 6th, 15th, 24th
Guide Numbers: 4, 9, 6

Home and family issues are highlighted. You could attend a gathering, visit a friend or relative in the hospital or help a loved one pick out something new. A small sacrifice of your time may be required when someone needs your compassion and understanding.

May 7th, 16th, 25th
Guide Numbers: 4, 9, 7

You could be disappointed about some aspect of a relationship, unsure of something in your career or upset because someone is trying to put you into a mold which you don't fit. Try not to put on an act in an attempt to please.

May 8th, 17th, 26th
Guide Numbers: 4, 9, 8

It is important that you find a positive channel for the determination you feel. With it you can accomplish anything you set your mind to. If your work is sedentary, some physical exercise could help rid you of your excess energy.

May 9th, 18th, 27th
Guide Numbers: 4, 9, 9

The 4 Year: Digging and Hoeing

You may find yourself wanting to get out of an undesirable situation: perhaps ending a relationship with an irresponsible lover or resigning from a boring job. Compassion for your fellow man could be an issue, and you may be instrumental in getting help for a person in need.

JUNE
Guide Numbers: 4, 1
Energy and confidence are high, making this a good time to start a new project or build a foundation for future goals. A personal decision needs to be made, and you may be called upon to take a leadership role in a minor crisis.

June 1st, 10th, 19th, 28th
Guide Numbers: 4, 1, 2
Delays can make you irritable, and you may have trouble controlling your temper when annoying details demand your time. "Haste makes waste" would be a good motto to keep in mind. Slowly but surely does it.

June 2nd, 11th, 20th, 29th
Guide Numbers: 4, 1, 3
You may be in an optimistic frame of mind and want to take action on an idea you've been mulling around. However, there are other things that require your attention as well. Jot down any brainstorms you don't have time to pursue at the present, so that you can go back to them at a later time.

June 3rd, 12th, 21st, 30th
Guide Numbers: 4, 1, 4
Practical matters are highlighted and could concern family, business, property or health. Make sure you are on time for all your appointments and stick to a budget. Try not to get discouraged if you feel limited or restricted in any way.

June 4th, 13th, 22nd
Guide Numbers: 4, 1, 5

The day's events are likely to take an unexpected turn: you could suddenly find yourself considering a change in plans. Although you may not be in the mood to wait for something you want, you would do well to consider long-range goals before acting on impulse.

June 5th, 14th, 23rd
Guide Numbers: 4, 1, 6

An event connected to home or family could cost you both time and money. You'll appreciate the loyalty and support of loved ones but won't want to bother with anyone who's unreliable or who makes you feel insecure.

June 6th, 15th, 24th
Guide Numbers: 4, 1, 7

You may feel like being left alone; your temper may be hard to control when someone close annoys you. You could find yourself making an effort to understand a person or situation you find confusing.

June 7th, 16th, 25th
Guide Numbers: 4, 1, 8

Be organized and efficient when putting your plans into action, or you may not have time to tend to all the things you need to do. Someone close to you may wait on you, rather than the other way around.

June 8th, 17th, 26th
Guide Numbers: 4, 1, 9

Something in your life may be in a state of transition, as one situation ends and another begins. If you don't adapt to change easily, it could be a bit disconcerting. Clear up any misunderstandings that may exist and focus on building new foundations for the future.

June 9th, 18th, 27th
Guide Numbers: 4, 1, 1

This is a good day to forge ahead where practical plans are concerned. Security, career advancement and general progress

The 4 Year: Digging and Hoeing

are likely to be on your mind, and it's important that you work toward the goals you've set.

JULY
Guide Numbers: 4, 2

Patience, tact and cooperation are the keynotes to progress this month. Even though delays can be frustrating, don't try to rush things or neglect details. Be sympathetic to the needs of loved ones—especially the elderly.

July 1st, 10th, 19th, 28th
Guide Numbers: 4, 2, 3

You may be feeling distracted and reluctant to deal with circumstances that press you for decisions or actions. However, don't pull the covers over your head. There is much to be done as well as to enjoy.

July 2nd, 11th, 20th, 29th
Guide Numbers: 4, 2, 4

You will need to be organized in order to accomplish everything in your schedule. Mundane chores cannot be avoided; you may feel bogged down by routine. This is a good time to straighten out the clutter on your desk, organize your briefcase or do the dishes that have piled up in the sink.

July 3rd, 12th, 21st, 30th
Guide Numbers: 4, 2, 5

Other people's reluctance to go along with your plans could be a source of frustration. New interests attract you, but you may wish to share them with loved ones rather than strike out on your own. Don't let lack of a co-adventurer impede your fun.

July 4th, 13th, 22nd, 31st
Guide Numbers: 4, 2, 6

You may feel burdened by some added responsibility. The work you do now will pay off later, but you may have to wait a while before seeing the results. Be patient and willing to make adjustments.

Your Daily Numerology

July 5th, 14th, 23rd
Guide Numbers: 4, 2, 7
   This is a good day to gather facts and scrutinize data of any kind. However, don't be too demanding or expect perfection. You are likely to be sensitive to criticism and may have a tendency to be critical yourself.

July 6th, 15th, 24th
Guide Numbers: 4, 2, 8
   Financial matters are highlighted: you may want to buy or sell something. Make sure you think before you act and exercise good judgment in *all* your decisions. Friends or co-workers may help you in some way, but you are really the one in control.

July 7th, 16th, 25th
Guide Numbers: 4, 2, 9
   Don't let yourself get bogged down in petty details. Try to see things from a broader scope. A loved one may need your compassion and understanding. Keep your mind open to differing points of view.

July 8th, 17th, 26th
Guide Numbers: 4, 2, 1
   Focus on goals for inner growth and career advancement. This is a good day to start a class, a home-improvement project or a new exercise program. Others will value your opinions: you may find yourself being the spokesperson for a group.

July 9th, 18th, 27th
Guide Numbers: 4, 2, 2
   You will need to cooperate with others and have much to gain by being tactful. Many little things can be attended to successfully, but be patient if they require more of your time than you anticipated.

AUGUST
Guide Numbers: 4, 3
   Creativity and self-expression are the keynotes to success this month. Although you still have many responsibilities, money

comes easier and you should be feeling more lighthearted. A short trip is likely. Be social and outgoing. People you meet may become important later.

August 1st, 10th, 19th, 28th
Guide Numbers: 4, 3, 4

A love interest may prove disappointing, or you may have the realization that not everyone is as reliable as you are. However, don't hold bitterness inside. If you air your upset with the one who caused it, you may discover that it was only a misunderstanding.

August 2nd, 11th, 20th, 29th
Guide Numbers: 4, 3, 5

You may find yourself doing a lot of coming and going. Take care not to spread yourself too thin. Ask yourself if all your projects and activities are worth your time and weed out those that aren't.

August 3rd, 12th, 21st, 30th
Guide Numbers: 4, 3, 6

Although you may be concerned about someone's health or well-being, worrying yourself about it won't do any good. Avoid being critical or giving unwanted advice. You could find yourself faced with an extra responsibility at home or at work. Accept it as a challenge.

August 4th, 13th, 22nd, 31st
Guide Numbers: 4, 3, 7

All may not be what it seems. Someone you are dealing with could leave out some pertinent information so that you don't get the full story. Make sure you look beneath the surface and read between the lines before jumping to conclusions.

August 5th, 14th, 23rd
Guide Numbers: 4, 3, 8

Business matters are likely to be on your mind: you may consider buying, selling or trading something. Make sure your finances are in order. If you have any outstanding debts, this is a good time to pay or collect them.

August 6th, 15th, 24th
Guide Numbers: 4, 3, 9

Tie up loose ends so that you're free to concentrate on important matters. Romance can be good if you and your partner are emotionally compatible; there can be a disagreement if you're not.

August 7th, 16th, 25th
Guide Numbers: 4, 3, 1

Something you've been planning may come to fruition and you'll have to decide where to go from here. Consider future security as well as present satisfaction. Charm could be an important asset.

August 8th, 17th, 26th
Guide Numbers: 4, 3, 2

This is a good day to get little things done. If you can work with others whose company you enjoy, your tasks won't seem so burdensome. You may feel a relationship growing deeper and becoming more meaningful, but don't try to rush things along.

August 9th, 18th, 27th
Guide Numbers: 4, 3, 3

Social contacts are important: someone you meet through a friend or co-worker could be influential in furthering your career. Make sure you write down any innovative ideas that come into your mind—you may not remember them tomorrow.

SEPTEMBER
Guide Numbers: 4, 4

Practical problems arise this month, testing your flexibility. Stick to all your schedules and keep within your budget. This is not a time to be frivolous, but try to be optimistic and think positive thoughts, rather than give in to depression. Rest, exercise and proper diet are important to your health.

September 1st, 10th, 19th, 28th
Guide Numbers: 4, 4, 5

The 4 Year: Digging and Hoeing

Unexpected problems are a source of tension and may disrupt your routine. Being careless or distracted could make you accident prone. Outdoor projects and physical activity are a good outlet for pent-up energy.

September 2nd, 11th, 20th, 29th
Guide Numbers: 4, 4, 6
Domestic responsibilities need your attention, and your career may also demand some extra effort. Unless you feel it's totally unfair, be willing to put in the additional time. You could be building a foundation for future security.

September 3rd, 12th, 21st, 30th
Guide Numbers: 4, 4, 7
Someone could annoy you and you may not know quite how to handle it. If you feel your privacy is being infringed upon or that a loved one is inconsiderate, try to discuss it calmly rather than give vent to a temperamental outburst.

September 4th, 13th, 22nd
Guide Numbers: 4, 4, 8
You will need to be organized and efficient. Make sure you have all the facts before making a decision; don't take anything for granted. Financial matters may require your attention: you would do well to exercise prudence and good judgment.

September 5th, 14th, 23rd
Guide Numbers: 4, 4, 9
This is a good day to finish some unfinished business. You may encounter a variety of emotions and should take care not to let jealousy or resentment gain the upper hand. There could be a disappointment where a personal relationship is concerned.

September 6th, 15th, 24th
Guide Numbers: 4, 4, 1
You may find yourself planning something that could affect your future. However, don't make commitments lightly. Someone new you meet through work is likely to be stable, reliable and around for a long time.

Your Daily Numerology

September 7th, 16th, 25th
Guide Numbers: 4, 4, 2

You are sensitive to little things, and expecting too much of others could prove disappointing. Those close to you may seem difficult to deal with, but attempts to force issues will only result in antagonizing them and prove a waste of time.

September 8th, 17th, 26th
Guide Numbers: 4, 4, 3

You may be feeling restless, but take care not to ignore long-term goals to gain short-term satisfaction. This is not a good time for capricious flirting. You would be better off sticking with someone tried and true.

September 9th, 18th, 27th
Guide Numbers: 4, 4, 4

Practical matters are highlighted, and you are likely to have much to concentrate on and put in order. Work hard and stick to your schedule, but try not to overdo it. Some time in the garden or fussing with plants could provide a refreshing interlude. A real estate matter may require your attention.

OCTOBER
Guide Numbers: 4, 5

Change is the keyword this month. You still have a lot to take care of, but there will also be an opportunity to get out and have some fun. New interests, new contacts and new activities are all highlighted, giving you much to think about. Something unexpected will come up to test your resourcefulness and adaptability. Don't be impulsive or argumentative and try to avoid hasty decisions.

October 1st, 10th, 19th, 28th
Guide Numbers: 4, 5, 6

Family affairs are highlighted: you could find yourself doing anything from taking the kids on an outing to entertaining at home or visiting a relative in the hospital. Duty to loved ones may interfere with your career.

The 4 Year: Digging and Hoeing

October 2nd, 11th, 20th, 29th
Guide Numbers: 4, 5, 7

You may not be feeling up to par; it's important that you get enough rest. An opportunity for a change in living conditions or occupation could come your way. Make sure you have all the information you need before making a decision.

October 3rd, 12th, 21st, 30th
Guide Numbers: 4, 5, 8

Business matters need tending to, and you will have to remain alert if you wish to make decisions that work to your best advantage. Weigh all the pros and cons carefully before taking action of any kind and don't let your emotions interfere with good judgment.

October 4th, 13th, 22nd, 31st
Guide Numbers: 4, 5, 9

You are likely to feel restless and confined unless you have a chance to do something different. Expand your horizons in some way; try to see things from a broader point of view. You could receive recognition for past efforts or hear from someone who's been away.

October 5th, 14th, 23rd
Guide Numbers: 4, 5, 1

Adventure may beckon in some form: you could find yourself exploring a new job, meeting a new romantic prospect or embarking on a trip. Make sure that any changes you make are a step forward, rather than a means of avoiding responsibility.

October 6th, 15th, 24th
Guide Numbers: 4, 5, 2

You may feel as though others have overlooked your interests, but try not to make mountains out of molehills or jump to hasty conclusions. Keeping your cool in the face of an upsetting situation can prevent it from mushrooming into something worse.

October 7th, 16th, 25th
Guide Numbers: 4, 5, 3

Your Daily Numerology

Communications are highlighted, and if deprived of social contacts you are likely to become bored or restless. A sudden urge to freshen up your surroundings may lead you to do some painting, rearrange the furniture or make a purchase for your home.

October 8th, 17th, 26th
Guide Numbers: 4, 5, 4

Chaotic surroundings or unpredictable situations are likely to make you uncomfortable. You may be concerned about an important change. This is a time to put things in order and build firm foundations for the future.

October 9th, 18th, 27th
Guide Numbers: 4, 5, 5

You may need to alter your plans due to an unforeseen event. A new person or scheme may seem alluring, but make sure you think before you act. Don't jeopardize the security you have now by doing something rash.

NOVEMBER
Guide Numbers: 4, 6

Domestic and/or business obligations that need to be taken care of could give rise to financial stress. Someone close to you may be hard to deal with and become a source of worry or frustration. You'll be faced with an important decision this month and may feel resentful about adjustments that have to be made. Try to take things as they come and keep your plans to yourself.

November 1st, 10th, 19th, 28th
Guide Numbers: 4, 6, 7

Mental pursuits are highlighted: you may learn a new skill that could help you on your job. Although it is good to be discriminating, try not to be overly critical or expect too much. There could be some emotional upset concerning a loved one.

November 2nd, 11th, 20th, 29th
Guide Numbers: 4, 6, 8

The 4 Year: Digging and Hoeing

You may be called upon to plan and arrange for others as well as for yourself. Try to act fairly in your dealings and avoid becoming headstrong. Don't let sentiment interfere with good judgment.

November 3rd, 12th, 21st, 30th
Guide Numbers: 4, 6, 9
Endings (not necessarily of a permanent nature) are highlighted, and you may have a hard time keeping your emotions in check. Although letting go of a situation or relationship may seem difficult, it could lead to an improved emotional outlook later.

November 4th, 13th, 22nd
Guide Numbers: 4, 6, 1
A new project could be on your mind. You may have to disregard what others say and do what you think is right, but try not to be dictatorial or insensitive in the process. Commitments or a broken promise could be an issue.

November 5th, 14th, 23rd
Guide Numbers: 4, 6, 2
Associations with others are highlighted. You may be feeling elated over a new romance or upset about one that doesn't seem to be working out. A compromise or sacrifice of some sort may be necessary in order to maintain peace and harmony in an important relationship.

November 6th, 15th, 24th
Guide Numbers: 4, 6, 3
This is a good day to be seen and heard but don't let social activities interfere with your responsibilities. You may be easily distracted, making it hard for you to concentrate on what you're doing.

November 7th, 16th, 25th
Guide Numbers: 4, 6, 4
The emphasis is on your home—cleaning it, repairing it, refurbishing it or even using it to entertain. However, obligations and responsibilities must also be met; you could feel burdened by the many demands of those close to you.

November 8th, 17th, 26th
Guide Numbers: 4, 6, 5

It may be difficult to predict the day's happenings or what you'll need when. Conflicting responsibilities are likely to test your flexibility and resourcefulness. You may experience unexpected problems in your relationships, at work as well as at home.

November 9th, 18th, 27th
Guide Numbers: 4, 6, 6

Domestic concerns are highlighted, and your mind may be on relationships (not necessarily your own). Don't fret if your attempts at matchmaking don't work out. Let nature take its course.

DECEMBER
Guide Numbers: 4, 7

Your life may seem quite complicated this month; you may feel like you're being pulled in many directions. Let others be of help rather than undertaking too much yourself. Although financial matters may be a source of frustration, have faith and try to stay calm. Things will be better next month if you don't push too hard now. Enjoy visits with loved ones who are supportive of you.

December 1st, 10th, 19th, 28th
Guide Numbers: 4, 7, 8

You may feel that someone has ulterior motives and because of it, be uneasy about not being in control. Don't let your emotions overrule common sense. Good judgment is a must. A past mistake may need to be accounted for and rectified.

December 2nd, 11th, 20th, 29th
Guide Numbers: 4, 7, 9

You may be feeling more generous and forgiving than usual and give someone the benefit of the doubt. Although this attitude is laudable, don't confuse being kind with being naive. Make sure you read the fine print on any papers that need to be signed.

December 3rd, 12th, 21st, 30th
Guide Numbers: 4, 7, 1

The 4 Year: Digging and Hoeing

You may feel like being left alone to pursue your own interests and are likely to resent any interruptions or demands. Take care not to become involved in anything of a shady nature.

December 4th, 13th, 22nd, 31st
Guide Numbers: 4, 7, 2

Try not to indulge in brooding or self-pity, even though you may feel lonely or misunderstood. This is not a time to jump to conclusions or let your imagination run wild. Dealings with an older woman could be in focus.

December 5th, 14th, 23rd
Guide Numbers: 4, 7, 3

This is a day to be social and outgoing; a short trip is a possibility. Emotions could be a problem unless you find some creative outlet through which to express them. Try jotting down your feelings and thoughts so you can make sense of them later.

December 6th, 15th, 24th
Guide Numbers: 4, 7, 4

You may have to come to grips with something beneath the surface that you've been hoping would go away. Health matters should not be ignored, no matter how insignificant they may seem. Try to spend some time outdoors.

December 7th, 16th, 25th
Guide Numbers: 4, 7, 5

You may be feeling restless and disconnected with your situation. However, avoid being hasty or impulsive or taking an unnecessary risk. A surprise call could change your mood.

December 8th, 17th, 26th
Guide Numbers: 4, 7, 6

Resentment or frustration could arise when someone close fails to do what you want or you are faced with numerous conflicting demands. Buying something new could give your spirits a lift—just keep your budget in mind.

December 9th, 18th, 27th
Guide Numbers: 4, 7, 7

Your Daily Numerology

The law of attraction is working for you: you may have an interesting enounter. Try to take irritations and annoyances in stride. Mental challenges will be stimulating, and you may benefit from knowledge you've studied or acquired.

CHAPTER SIX

THE 5 YEAR

"Budding Time"

GUIDE NUMBER: 5
COLOR: LIGHT BLUE

This is the year to flow with changing conditions, live on a day-to-day basis and learn to let go. It will be a fast-paced period and you should expect the unexpected. Sudden reversals from good to bad or bad to good are not uncommon. You may be feeling restless, impetuous and more adventuresome than usual, and you could have trouble concentrating on one thing at a time. Take care not to let distractions make you accident prone.

This is a time to have fun, speculate, take a trip, be active and enjoy the sensual pleasures of life (without overdoing it, of course). Get out and circulate, promote yourself and your ideas, eliminate the boring and monotonous from your life. Explore new things. Your personal magnetism and sex appeal are high; you may become involved in a transitory romance. Those of you with a weight or drinking problem may have trouble keeping it under control, as self-discipline is likely to be difficult to maintain.

Success and happiness come through being adaptable, growing, expanding and picking up unexpected opportunities before they are lost. Avoid neglecting responsibilities, procrastinating, overindulging in sensual activities and misusing your personal freedom at the expense of others.

Your Daily Numerology

JANUARY
Guide Numbers: 5, 6

Duties and responsibilities take up much of your time this month, leaving you very little for yourself. Although you have to make many adjustments for those close to you, and their demands may seem excessive, try not to let resentment build up. Sympathy and patience achieve better results than hasty words or deeds.

January 1st, 10th, 19th, 28th
Guide Numbers: 5, 6, 7

There may be some misunderstanding between you and a loved one, and unless you are clear about what you mean, your words could be misinterpreted. This is a good time to catch up on reading any magazines or papers that have been accumulating.

January 2nd, 11th, 20th, 29th
Guide Numbers: 5, 6, 8

Business matters are highlighted; you may become very conscious of your status. There could be someone you want to impress. An important decision could entail extra responsibility.

January 3rd, 12th, 21st, 30th
Guide Numbers: 5, 6, 9

Try not to meddle or force your ideas on others, lest it result in tension or a clash of wills. Being considerate and a good listener is more advantageous. You may have to let go of something that you've been reluctant to part with.

January 4th, 13th, 22nd, 31st
Guide Numbers: 5, 6, 1

This is a good day to try something new with your family or friends. You may have a brainstorm for improving your domestic situation, but take care to present it as a suggestion rather than a decree.

January 5th, 14th, 23rd
Guide Numbers: 5, 6, 2

You may find yourself having to make an adjustment at home—giving up your bed to an overnight guest or agreeing to watch a TV program that was second choice with you. Be willing

The 5 Year: Budding Time

to compromise. Quarrels will get you nowhere, but unselfishness will be rewarded.

January 6th, 15th, 24th
Guide Numbers: 5, 6, 3

Music plays a part in your life, even it it's only singing in the shower. Try to keep your mind on what you're doing or distractions will make you careless. If you're in the market for a new romance, chances of meeting someone at a social function are good.

January 7th, 16th, 25th
Guide Numbers: 5, 6, 4

Many demands are made on your time and energy; you may feel limited by family or career responsibilities. Your home is likely to be on your mind—possibly in connection with a move.

January 8th, 17th, 26th
Guide Numbers: 5, 6, 5

Relationships are in focus, whether it's starting a new one or getting rid of the old. Change is in the air—you may be in for a surprise. A blind date may not turn out the way you anticipated.

January 9th, 18th, 27th
Guide Numbers: 5, 6, 6

An obligation could interfere with your personal plans—a compromise may be necessary. If someone seeks your advice, state your opinion objectively without getting emotionally involved.

FEBRUARY
Guide Numbers: 5, 7

It is important to get enough rest this month and to avoid excessive worrying. Even though situations around you may not be entirely to your liking, this is not a good time to force any issues. Try to analyze your problems without getting emotional. You may be presented with the opportunity to pursue a new study.

February 1st, 10th, 19th, 28th
Guide Numbers: 5, 7, 8

Your Daily Numerology

Recognition for knowledge you've acquired could come your way. Don't be shy about accepting a compliment. Financial matters will need your attention: you may have to take care of an unexpected expense.

February 2nd, 11th, 20th, 29th
Guide Numbers: 5, 7, 9
You may feel restless and not know why. Change is in the air and it would benefit you to be broad-minded and open to new people, places and ideas. Don't cling to something that has become unsatisfactory just because of its familiarity.

February 3rd, 12th, 21st
Guide Numbers: 5, 7, 1
Mental pursuits are favored, and you are likely to seek out people who can teach you something new. Freedom to do your own thing is important now; you are bound to be irritated by any interference with your plans.

February 4th, 13th, 22nd
Guide Numbers: 5, 7, 2
Details may need to be ironed out. It is a good time to do research or gather information. Unexpected delays could be a source of frustration. Try to take them in your stride.

February 5th, 14th, 23rd
Guide Numbers: 5, 7, 3
Games of chance are likely to appeal to you, whether it be handicapping a race or merely psyching out the boss. You may be tempted to go on a shopping spree and could wind up spending more than you planned.

February 6th, 15th, 24th
Guide Numbers: 5, 7, 4
You may have difficulty understanding what makes certain people tick. Make sure you think things through before jumping to conclusions. Vituperative arguments could cause digestive upsets or a "what's-the-use" attitude.

The 5 Year: Budding Time

February 7th, 16th, 25th
Guide Numbers: 5, 7, 5
You're kidding yourself if you think it will be easy to keep a relationship strictly platonic. Sensual pleasures are highlighted, and it may take all the self-discipline you can muster not to overindulge.

February 8th, 17th, 26th
Guide Numbers: 5, 7, 6
This is a good day to catch up on chores at home and at work. A battle of wills could result if you try to force your ideas on others. Be willing to compromise and reconcile differences.

February 9th, 18th, 27th
Guide Numbers: 5, 7, 7
You may be feeling misunderstood or confused about an important relationship, but this is not a good time to try and force issues. Spend some time alone reading, writing down your thoughts or just planning a course of action for the future.

MARCH
Guide Numbers: 5, 8
Efficiency and good judgment are the keynotes to success and happiness this month. Don't postpone business matters or let obstacles stand in your way. This is a time to put your plans into action without delay. Those in a position of authority can be helpful. Your finances are likely to improve, but expenses may also be high.

March 1st, 10th, 19th, 28th
Guide Numbers: 5, 8, 9
Hearing from an old love or business associate could lead to some nostalgic moments, but don't let yourself become maudlin over the past. You may have to give up something or sever a tie in order to leave yourself free for a new opportunity.

Your Daily Numerology

March 2nd, 11th, 20th, 29th
Guide Numbers: 5, 8, 1

Don't let preoccupation over a personal concern prevent you from getting out and exploring new things. Prospects for romance are good, and you could have a productive business encounter as well.

March 3rd, 12th, 21st, 30th
Guide Numbers: 5, 8, 2

Companionship is highlighted: a friend may require cheering up. However, you are very vulnerable to your surroundings, so make sure it's you who changes your friend's mood and not the other way around.

March 4th, 13th, 22nd, 31st
Guide Numbers: 5, 8, 3

Communications are highlighted: you are likely to get an interesting letter or phone call. If you are faced with a business decision, be careful not to get into something that looks good but may prove burdensome later.

March 5th, 14th, 23rd
Guide Numbers: 5, 8, 4

This is a day to plan for the future. Think of ways to get ahead and take action to change whatever you are not satisfied with in your life. Accept a challenge and prove that you can do it.

March 6th, 15th, 24th
Guide Numbers: 5, 8, 5

You may find a business or personal difficulty resolved, and an unexpected raise or opportunity for additional income could come your way. If you feel tempted to gamble on some new investment, make sure you take the cons into consideration along with the pros.

March 7th, 16th, 25th
Guide Numbers: 5, 8, 6

Adjustments may be necessary due to some conflict between your domestic responsibilities and your career. An important decision has to be made—possibly in connection with your home.

The 5 Year: Budding Time

March 8th, 17th, 26th
Guide Numbers: 5, 8, 7

This is a good day to organize your affairs and think about changes you'd like to make. If you have to sign any papers, make sure you read between the lines. There could be more beneath the surface than what's immediately apparent.

March 9th, 18th, 27th
Guide Numbers: 5, 8, 8

Good judgment is important, especially where spending money is concerned. Try not to be unnecessarily extravagant. This is a time to put your plans into action, but don't take advantage of others in the process.

APRIL
Guide Numbers: 5, 9

Travel plans are in the air, but so are frustrating circumstances. A certain situation comes to an end and legalities may require your attention. Don't be surprised if you find yourself in different surroundings for a while.

April 1st, 10th, 19th, 28th
Guide Numbers: 5, 9, 1

Energy is high, making this a good day to promote yourself and your ideas. Someone new could enter your life through some activity you both share—perhaps a political club, a consciousness-raising group or a tour.

April 2nd, 11th, 20th, 29th
Guide Numbers: 5, 9, 2

This is a day that could play like a soap opera if you let your emotions get out of hand. Detach yourself and try to see trying circumstances from an objective point of view. If necessary, put yourself in the other person's shoes.

April 3rd, 12th, 21st, 30th
Guide Numbers: 5, 9, 3

Energy and optimism are high; it's a good day to spend with friends and children. You may have a hard time keeping your mind on routine work, or it may catch fire and be creative—either way, you could wind up spending much longer on a project than you should.

April 4th, 13th, 22nd
Guide Numbers: 5, 9, 4
Your moods may be very changeable, running the gamut from enthusiasm to depression and back again. Not knowing how a pending event will turn out could put your nerves on edge. Try to take things in stride and think positive thoughts.

April 5th, 14th, 23rd
Guide Numbers: 5, 9, 5
You are likely to be influenced by new interests and people. Inner unrest could lead you to be hasty or impulsive, and you should take care not to let unexpected problems in a personal relationship lead to an outburst of temper you may regret later.

April 6th, 15th, 24th
Guide Numbers: 5, 9, 6
Family matters are highlighted; you may resent having to attend some function that doesn't appeal to you. If you try to force your ideas on those close to you, a clash of wills could result. Be willing to adjust and reconcile differences.

April 7th, 16th, 25th
Guide Numbers: 5, 9, 7
There may be some tension between you and a loved one unless channels of communication are open on both sides. If something bothers you, it's best to talk about it rather than keep it bottled up inside.

April 8th, 17th, 26th
Guide Numbers: 5, 9, 8
You'll need to use good judgment as you tend to affairs. A legal matter could require your attention, or you may be involved in an important sale. Indecision as to the right course of action could be a source of frustration; you would be wise to seek an expert's advice.

The 5 Year: Budding Time

April 9th, 18th, 27th
Guide Numbers: 5, 9, 9

You may be feeling surprisingly emotional and spend much of the day thinking and remembering as some old aspect of your life is brought to an end. This is a good time to broaden your scope of interests. Once you put the past behind you, new channels open up.

MAY
Guide Numbers: 5, 1

A surprise turn of events could create a new opportunity for you this month. Take advantage of it. If you're in a rut, this is the time to make changes. Meet new people and explore new ideas. Do your own thing but avoid irresponsible behavior.

May 1st, 10th, 19th, 28th
Guide Numbers: 5, 1, 2

Today could be the turning point in a relationship, or an association with someone you've just met may become more important in your life. An unexpected delay could be a source of frustration, but don't let it make you overanxious.

May 2nd, 11th, 20th, 29th
Guide Numbers: 5, 1, 3

You'll probably feel optimistic and enthusiastic and be eager to move forward with your plans. However, don't feel offended if no one else is as gung ho as you are. It might be a good idea not to talk too much about what's going on in your personal life.

May 3rd, 12th, 21st, 30th
Guide Numbers: 5, 1, 4

Practical matters are highlighted. It's a time to meet your obligations and organize your affairs. If you make a positive effort to clear away any obstacles in your path, you can forge ahead and begin to change things.

May 4th, 13th, 22nd, 31st
Guide Numbers: 5, 1, 5

Your Daily Numerology

This is a good day to promote yourself and your ideas. Change is in the air, and you could feel a bit uncertain as to which of many possible roads you should follow. New people may enter your life; you could find yourself enjoying something you never thought you'd try.

May 5th, 14th, 23rd
Guide Numbers: 5, 1, 6
A domestic or community responsibility will require your attention. You may wind up having to play the role of mediator, but try not to interfere unless you are asked. Giving unwanted advice could backfire in your face.

May 6th, 15th, 24th
Guide Numbers: 5, 1, 7
You need some time to be by yourself, away from the rat race and people who make demands on you. If it's impossible to be alone, try to shut out the chaos for a while so that you can analyze, reflect and think. Read the fine print on papers that need to be signed.

May 7th, 16th, 25th
Guide Numbers: 5, 1, 8
Freedom to do what you want with your time may be an issue when someone in your life tries to tell you what to do. Although you should meet opposition to your plans firmly and decisively, use tact rather than belligerence to gain your ends.

May 8th, 17th, 26th
Guide Numbers: 5, 1, 9
You'll be anxious to finish your work and pursue some leisure-time activity. Sentimental and romantic feelings may lead you to indulge in a flight of fantasy. You will probably rather be with a lover than with friends.

May 9th, 18th, 27th
Guide Numbers: 5, 1, 1
You'll feel like doing things on your own without interference from others and may be unduly annoyed if someone fouls up your plans. This is a good time to promote yourself, be crea-

The 5 Year: Budding Time

tive or ask for what you want. However, don't expect everything to happen at once.

JUNE
Guide Numbers: 5, 2

Patience, tact and diplomacy are the keynotes to success and happiness this month. Although those close to you may seem difficult to deal with, and annoying delays are likely to be a source of frustration, it's not advisable to force issues at this time. Don't give in to the temptation to ignore boring details—they could be more important than you think.

June 1st, 10th, 19th, 28th
Guide Numbers: 5, 2, 3

The law of attraction is working for you. If you're unattached, a fresh outlook could bring someone new into your life. Being in the right place at the right time doesn't hurt, either. Get out there and circulate!

June 2nd, 11th, 20th, 29th
Guide Numbers: 5, 2, 4

If you've been discouraged lately, it's a good day to take care of details and get things done. All those chores that have been allowed to pile up can be cleared away with a little determination on your part.

June 3rd, 12th, 21st, 30th
Guide Numbers: 5, 2, 5

It's important to keep your mind on what you're doing, or you could be in for an unpleasant surprise. Daydreaming at the wrong time is likely to result in a careless mistake. It's a good time to go on a short trip with a loved one or spend some time at your favorite sport.

June 4th, 13th, 22nd
Guide Numbers: 5, 2, 6

Events or people will cause you to make some adjustments, and you may encounter a delay in your plans or incur an added expense or responsibility. Your patience could be sorely tested by the actions of a relative or friend.

June 5th, 14th, 23rd
Guide Numbers: 5, 2, 7

You could be feeling fussy about where you spend your time and whom you spend it with. Your vitality may be lower than usual, making you want to catch up on your rest. However, if someone important extends an invitation to do something you think you'd enjoy, you are likely to be able to summon up the energy and go.

June 6th, 15th, 24th
Guide Numbers: 5, 2, 8

Someone in a position of authority may try to talk you into something. If you have any doubts about it, make sure you investigate further before committing yourself. Don't underestimate the importance of small details. They may not be as insignificant as they seem.

June 7th, 16th, 25th
Guide Numbers: 5, 2, 9

Trying circumstances could be frustrating; you may be more temperamental than usual. Take care to avoid an emotional outburst. However, reminiscing with an old friend could put you in a nostalgic mood.

June 8th, 17th, 26th
Guide Numbers: 5, 2, 1

Today can bring varied activities—anything from a new partnership opportunity to a romantic encounter. Although it's a good time to forge ahead with your plans, there are others you have to consider. Be tactful and willing to cooperate.

June 9th, 18th, 27th
Guide Numbers: 5, 2, 2

Your patience is likely to be tested. A person or situation could annoy you, or there may be a delay that sets your nerves on edge. Count to ten before snapping at anyone and guard against being oversensitive.

The 5 Year: Budding Time

JULY
Guide Numbers: 5, 3

Ideas come fast and furious and could result in improved conditions if followed up. However, avoid impulsiveness, extravagance or scattering your energies in too many directions. Romance and travel are in the air, making this a good month for taking a vacation and mixing with others. Socializing can lead to an unexpected opportunity, but remember that careless words may be misinterpreted.

July 1st, 10th, 19th, 28th
Guide Numbers: 5, 3, 4

This is a good day to come down to earth and put your ideas into concrete form. Be practical and realistic. Remain alert to opportunities that may come your way. Remember that a positive disposition can attract pleasant happenings.

July 2nd, 11th, 20th, 29th
Guide Numbers: 5, 3, 5

Take care not to be so busy thinking about other things that you forget an important detail, such as making sure you have enough money in your account before you write a check or watching the traffic lights before you make a turn. Being careless or distracted could make you accident prone.

July 3rd, 12th, 21st, 30th
Guide Numbers: 5, 3, 6

Social activities and domestic chores are in focus. You may be doing some entertaining or going on a family outing. Be willing to compromise and make adjustments.

July 4th, 13th, 22nd, 31st
Guide Numbers: 5, 3, 7

You could be feeling a bit out of sorts because of the behavior of a friend or loved one. Try not to take everything personally and read meanings into things that aren't there.

July 5th, 14th, 23rd
Guide Numbers: 5, 3, 8

Your Daily Numerology

You'll want to have control over your affairs and may resent being told what to do or not do. However, get expert advice before rushing headlong into what seems like a good opportunity. Business and pleasure can be successfully combined.

July 6th, 15th, 24th
Guide Numbers: 5, 3, 9

There is something you may want to have done with so that you can go on to other things. Romance is highlighted: those who are single could meet a new love. However, don't expect it to turn into a long-term relationship.

July 7th, 16th, 25th
Guide Numbers: 5, 3, 1

This is a good day to start a vacation or try some new form of recreation. An idea or inspiration could put you in an optimistic mood. Someone you meet is likely to prove important later on.

July 8th, 17th, 26th
Guide Numbers: 5, 3, 2

Associations with others are highlighted, and you may not have time to tend to all the little things you want to do. Someone close to you could require special handling, or a friendship may turn into romance if the setting is right.

July 9th, 18th, 27th
Guide Numbers: 5, 3, 3

This is a good day to make new friends, be creative and express your opinions and ideas. You are likely to find yourself the center of attention at some point. Social activities are highlighted; something beneficial could come to you through someone you meet.

AUGUST
Guide Numbers: 5, 4

Practical problems must be faced and financial decisions made. Although you may have a strong desire to move ahead, you are likely to feel constrained by the demands of others. Responsi-

The 5 Year: Budding Time

bilities need to be shouldered and obstacles plowed through. Success comes from meeting difficulty calmly and ingeniously. Tension can affect your health.

August 1st, 10th, 19th, 28th
Guide Numbers: 5, 4, 5

Your adaptability and resourcefulness may be put to the test when something fails to turn out the way you planned. Unexpected twists and turns are likely, and you could bump into someone you've been out of touch with for a while.

August 2nd, 11th, 20th, 29th
Guide Numbers: 5, 4, 6

Home and family demands could interfere with your career or social life and cause you to feel frustrated or restricted. Try to organize your day as efficiently as possible and avoid taking on more than your fair share of responsibilities.

August 3rd, 12th, 21st, 30th
Guide Numbers: 5, 4, 7

Don't let outward appearances or first impressions deceive you or you may miss an opportunity. Unless you are on the alert and willing to look beneath the surface, you could fail to recognize a diamond in the rough.

August 4th, 13th, 22nd, 31st
Guide Numbers: 5, 4, 8

You may have to handle a challenge. Good judgment and efficiency will pay off. Don't let matters drift or obstacles stand in your way. Some unexpected expenses may need to be taken care of: you could experience some financial strain.

August 5th, 14th, 23rd
Guide Numbers: 5, 4, 9

Be prepared to buckle down and work. Think before you act and you may avoid doing something foolish just out of boredom. Loose ends need to be tied up. This is a good time to get rid of things that have outlived their usefulness.

Your Daily Numerology

August 6th, 15th, 24th
Guide Numbers: 5, 4, 1

A new opportunity may come your way but it will require hard work and sound foundations to see it to fruition. Be enterprising and constructive. Do what *you* think is right.

August 7th, 16th, 25th
Guide Numbers: 5, 4, 2

You are likely to undergo some emotional strain—a friend may expect you to listen to more than you care to hear, or something may not materialize the way you hoped. Details must be attended to now; patience is your best resort.

August 8th, 17th, 26th
Guide Numbers: 5, 4, 3

Hard work could be interrupted by something lighthearted and fun. However, don't let yourself get carried away. Practical matters still require your attention, and you should strive for balance between work and play.

August 9th, 18th, 27th
Guide Numbers: 5, 4, 4

This is a good day to do something with your hands: scrub a floor, do some carpentry, take care of your plants. Concentrate on being practical and get things organized and cleared away.

SEPTEMBER
Guide Numbers: 5, 5

Your personal freedom is highlighted this month. Try to direct change, not resist it. As you become involved in new interests and activities, you may suddenly find yourself freed from an old condition or responsibility. Don't take criticism to heart or be quick to start an argument. Moderation is advisable now. Willpower is low, however, and you could wind up overindulging.

September 1st, 10th, 19th, 28th
Guide Numbers: 5, 5, 6

The 5 Year: Budding Time

You may not have much time for yourself. Others could ask you to help them out, and domestic responsibilities are likely to crop up. If you feel you are being imposed upon or taken advantage of, draw the line firmly but tactfully.

September 2nd, 11th, 20th, 29th
Guide Numbers: 5, 5, 7
Try not to wallow in depressing thoughts. Reading a new book, going to a show or lecture on a subject that interests you or even trying a new delicacy from the gourmet shop could improve your mood. Be careful of losing money from your pocket or purse. Make sure you count your change.

September 3rd, 12th, 21st, 30th
Guide Numbers: 5, 5, 8
You may be faced with an unexpected decision, such as changing jobs or moving. Consider long-term goals as well as short-term profits. Someone in a position of influence may play an important part in the day's events.

September 4th, 13th, 22nd
Guide Numbers: 5, 5, 9
You are likely to be feeling restless and may resent anyone or anything that curbs your freedom. This is a good time to take a vacation or embark on a trip. You could have an urge to change something in your environment and may unexpectedly find yourself freed from an undesirable situation.

September 5th, 14th, 23rd
Guide Numbers: 5, 5, 1
New people, new activities and new opportunities are highlighted. The day could mark a turning point in some area of your life. This is a good time to promote yourself and your ideas. Change is in the air: something you've been waiting for may come about.

September 6th, 15th, 24th
Guide Numbers: 5, 5, 2
Little things that seem like a nuisance will have to be dealt with. Take care not to overlook an important detail. Companion-

ship is important: an evening spent with friends would be preferable to being by yourself.

September 7th, 16th, 25th
Guide Numbers: 5, 5, 3

You may have a hard time concentrating on any one thing and should avoid spreading yourself too thin. Keep your mind on what you're doing or you may make a careless mistake. Some unexpected news could come your way.

September 8th, 17th, 26th
Guide Numbers: 5, 5, 4

Obstacles may seem to pop out of nowhere, and something could fail to materialize the way you had hoped. You may suddenly find yourself brought down to earth by some practical issue that forces you to change your plans or approach.

September 9th, 18th, 27th
Guide Numbers: 5, 5, 5

You are likely to be full of restless energy and should take care not to become so scattered that you overlook an opportunity that may come your way. Unexpected twists and turns will test your ability to adjust and be resourceful.

OCTOBER
Guide Numbers: 5, 6

Trying to balance your personal life and obligations to others could be frustrating this month. Be helpful to those who seek your assistance, but don't undertake more than you can comfortably handle or allow yourself to be imposed upon. Domestic and community matters are highlighted; you may be inspired to do some entertaining at home.

October 1st, 10th, 19th, 28th
Guide Numbers: 5, 6, 7

Strive to understand yourself and others today and bring disagreements out into the open rather than let mistaken assumptions get you down. Openness and honesty in your personal relationships can avert harbored resentments on either side.

The 5 Year: Budding Time

October 2nd, 11th, 20th, 29th
Guide Numbers: 5, 6, 8

Family or business matters will require your attention. You'll need to be organized and efficient. Money may be an issue, and there could be a disagreement or confusion about what something costs.

October 3rd, 12th, 21st, 30th
Guide Numbers: 5, 6, 9

There may be some tension between yourself and a family member. Although you could have a difficult time keeping your emotions in check, you have more to gain by being tolerant and compassionate than by being temperamental or possessive.

October 4th, 13th, 22nd, 31st
Guide Numbers: 5, 6, 1

You may decide to add something new to your home or think up an activity the whole family could enjoy. Take care not to be so busy with your plans that you overlook the feelings of someone close to you.

October 5th, 14th, 23rd
Guide Numbers: 5, 6, 2

You may become involved in a domestic quarrel, either as a participant or a mediator. Be willing to listen to what others have to say, even if you feel you are being treated unfairly. Adjustments to those close to you will prove necessary.

October 6th, 15th, 24th
Guide Numbers: 5, 6, 3

You will probably be in the mood for socializing; an invitation could be hard to turn down. It's okay to enjoy yourself, but don't neglect your responsibilities.

October 7th, 16th, 25th
Guide Numbers: 5, 6, 4

You are likely to feel burdened by a career responsibility or family concern. Being unrealistic in your expectations could lead to disappointment when someone close to you fails to act the way you think they should.

Your Daily Numerology

October 8th, 17th, 26th
Guide Numbers: 5, 6, 5
　　Today could mark a turning point in an important relationship. Those who are single could meet a new love. However, people with partners who jump to hasty conclusions or are unwilling to make adjustments may find trouble ahead.

October 9th, 18th, 27th
Guide Numbers: 5, 6, 6
　　You may be feeling some concern about a loved one or find yourself performing a service of some kind. Family and community responsibilities are in focus, and you could have to rearrange your schedule around them.

NOVEMBER
Guide Numbers: 5, 7
　　Rest and some time alone are important to your well-being this month. Concentrate on yourself rather than becoming involved in other people's problems. Misunderstandings can be avoided if you take the time to think things out and put them in their proper perspective. Take a course or do something to improve your skills.

November 1st, 10th, 19th, 28th
Guide Numbers: 5, 7, 8
　　Past mistakes may have to be accounted for and rectified. Do what you can to eliminate clutter in your surroundings and organize your affairs so that you don't waste time. A situation that requires quick thinking and immediate action could arise.

November 2nd, 11th, 20th, 29th
Guide Numbers: 5, 7, 9
　　You are susceptible to upsets and aggravations. Traffic jams, nosy neighbors or cheap companions may get on your nerves. Try to be tolerant and understanding and keep an open mind.

November 3rd, 12th, 21st, 30th
Guide Numbers: 5, 7, 1

The 5 Year: Budding Time

Being free to do what you want when you want to is important; you may resent anyone ordering you around. You could find yourself planning a short trip due to some unexpected news.

November 4th, 13th, 22nd
Guide Numbers: 5, 7, 2

There could be deceit in your dealings with others; some person or situation may require patience and diplomacy. Be adaptable to cancelled plans or changes in your schedule, irritating though they may be. There is nothing you can do to push matters along for the time being.

November 5th, 14th, 23rd
Guide Numbers: 5, 7, 3

You are likely to be more conscious than usual of how things look: if you make a purchase now you will want it to be of good quality and style. Some surprise news concerning a pet or child could be the highlight of your day.

November 6th, 15th, 24th
Guide Numbers: 5, 7, 4

You may not be feeling up to par. Unexpected problems may upset you at work or you may find the conversation or behavior of someone close to you bewildering. Try to get to the bottom of any misunderstanding.

November 7th, 16th, 25th
Guide Numbers: 5, 7, 5

A feeling of restlessness prevails. You would do well to avoid impulsive words or actions which may be regretted later. Sensual pleasures are highlighted, and your willpower is likely to be low.

November 8th, 17th, 26th
Guide Numbers: 5, 7, 6

Doing your own thing may be difficult: you are likely to have to make some adjustments at home or at work. An important relationship may run into problems if you are critical or insist you are right all the time.

November 9th, 18th, 27th
Guide Numbers: 5, 7, 7

You may feel that others don't understand you or that your needs are being overlooked. Try to concentrate on positive things rather than wallow in negativity. Mental stimulation is important.

DECEMBER
Guide Numbers: 5, 8

Material affairs are highlighted this month: some unexpected gain could come your way. Improved finances give you more freedom to do the things you want. However, unforeseen expenses may also have to be taken care of, so try not to get carried away with spending.

December 1st, 10th, 19th, 28th
Guide Numbers: 5, 8, 9

Some matter may need to be settled, such as a legal issue or a project at work. Although you are likely to be very busy, try not to be short with someone who is not moving as fast as you would like.

December 2nd, 11th, 20th, 29th
Guide Numbers: 5, 8, 1

Action leads to success, especially where business matters are concerned. Don't waste time on anything unproductive. A promotion or an opportunity to increase your finances may be highlighted. If you are involved in competitive sports you could find yourself in the lead, but be a good sport if you don't.

December 3rd, 12th, 21st, 30th
Guide Numbers: 5, 8, 2

Don't be arrogant or pushy or try to do everything yourself. Others will have to be accommodated if you are to get what you want. Someone in a position of authority could be a source of good advice.

December 4th, 13th, 22nd, 31st
Guide Numbers: 5, 8, 3

Communications are highlighted: you are likely to do a great deal of talking. However, take care to avoid saying too much. You may discover you are the recipient of an unexpected gift.

The 5 Year: Budding Time

December 5th, 14th, 23rd
Guide Numbers: 5, 8, 4
    Practical matters may require your attention, but don't let them get in the way of any planning for the future. Use your wits to engineer a course of action that will be conducive to getting what you want, and meet opposition with calmness and ingenuity.

December 6th, 15th, 24th
Guide Numbers: 5, 8, 5
    Don't expect things to go off like clockwork. You could be in for a surprise. This is a time to be adaptable and versatile. Alertness and resourcefulness could lead to gain.

December 7th, 16th, 25th
Guide Numbers: 5, 8, 6
    Family matters are likely to conflict with your career; there may be some adjustment or compromise you have to make. An important decision could be on your mind, or some extra expense involving your home or a loved one could come up.

December 8th, 17th, 26th
Guide Numbers: 5, 8, 7
    All may not be as it seems, and you should be aware that there can be more to a situation than meets the eye. Make sure you get expert advice and read the fine print before signing papers or contracts of any kind.

December 9th, 18th, 27th
Guide Numbers: 5, 8, 8
    Someone in a position of authority could be helpful. You may not feel like being restricted or being told what to do, but good judgment is still a must. Take care not to overspend and try not to be insensitive to others.

CHAPTER SEVEN

THE 6 YEAR

"The Blossoming Time"

GUIDE NUMBER: 6
COLOR: INDIGO or ROYAL BLUE

This is a year to settle down, accept responsibility and fulfill your obligations. Relationships are likely to be more stable; it is one of the best times for marriage. Your interests are likely to center around your home, family and community, and you will be more willing to make adjustments and compromises to the needs of those you love.

This is the time to follow through with your commitments and clear up misunderstandings. Be a guide to your children and a host to your friends, move into a new home or redecorate the one you have. Join a committee; collect debts owed to you and also be sure to pay the ones you owe. Be helpful to those close to you, but try to avoid meddling in their affairs or giving unwanted advice. It is important to be open to differing points of view and let the other person be right once in a while.

Harmony is the keynote of the year; success and happiness come through unselfish duty to family and community. Avoid being domineering, argumentative and expecting too much from others.

JANUARY
Guide Numbers: 6, 7

Frustration results when you encounter obstacles to your plans or seem to be getting little reward for much effort and hard work. However, try not to push too hard for action at the moment. It pays to be patient and think things through before you act. A health matter (not necessarily your own) could be a source of worry. Make sure you get enough rest.

January 1st, 10th, 19th, 28th
Guide Numbers: 6, 7, 8
Financial matters are highlighted: it's a good time to pay bills or take care of your banking. Should you have a disagreement with a loved one over money, try to work it out logically and don't let your emotions rule your head.

January 2nd, 11th, 20th, 29th
Guide Numbers: 6, 7, 9
You are likely to be in a critical mood today and may have a hard time controlling your temper. Try not to take offense if your ideas aren't readily accepted by others. You may be faced with an upsetting conclusion of some kind.

January 3rd, 12th, 21st, 30th
Guide Numbers: 6, 7, 1
Don't waste energy worrying over family problems you can't do anything about. Although you may have some ideas as to what should be done, try to avoid headstrong tactics. Being pushy or stubborn gets you nowhere.

January 4th, 13th, 22nd, 31st
Guide Numbers: 6, 7, 2
Oversensitivity could be a problem; you may be feeling touchy or out of sorts. Try not to let domestic hassles get you down. A compromise may be necessary in order to get what you want.

January 5th, 14th, 23rd
Guide Numbers: 6, 7, 3
This is a good day to spend with friends; a social event could be fun. Try to avoid gossip or jumping to hasty conclusions. A child or pet may need special attention.

The 6 Year: The Blossoming Time

January 6th, 15th, 24th
Guide Numbers: 6, 7, 4
It may be difficult juggling career and domestic duties, but if you are organized and efficient, you'll be amazed at how much you can accomplish. This is a good time to gather facts or do research for a project at work or school.

January 7th, 16th, 25th
Guide Numbers: 6, 7, 5
Before you agree to do a favor for someone, make sure you know all the facts. It could entail more than you think. If you enjoy sports or playing cards, today could be a good day to get involved in a game.

January 8th, 17th, 26th
Guide Numbers: 6, 7, 6
Domestic matters are likely to haunt you: you'll have to do certain chores whether you want to or not. Complaining about your responsibilities won't make them go away. The sooner you get to them, the faster they'll get done.

January 9th, 18th, 27th
Guide Numbers: 6, 7, 7
Someone overcritical could make you tense and edgy. Try to take irritations and annoyances in your stride. Be sure you read the fine print before signing anything.

FEBRUARY
Guide Numbers: 6, 8
Organization and good judgment are this month's keynotes to success and happiness. Finances are in focus, and you may be embarking on a business trip. A property matter or investment may also require your attention. You have a lot to do, so budget your time as well as your money.

February 1st, 10th, 19th, 28th
Guide Numbers: 6, 8, 9
A family, business or legal matter may require your attention. Use good judgment and don't let your emotions rule your head.

Your Daily Numerology

Try to understand all sides of the issue rather than insist on your own point of view.

February 2nd, 11th, 20th, 29th
Guide Numbers: 6, 8, 1

Energy and confidence are high, making this a good day to tackle responsibilities in your business and personal life. You are apt to put your own interests first, which is fine so long as no one else suffers for it.

February 3rd, 12th, 21st
Guide Numbers: 6, 8, 2

You are more willing to fuss over loved ones, but you'll also expect your efforts to be reciprocated. This is a good day to take care of all those little details that need doing and that seem to take up so much time.

February 4th, 13th, 22nd
Guide Numbers: 6, 8, 3

This is a good day to circulate and be seen and heard. Be sure you look your best. Try not to be extravagant or impulsive where your finances are concerned.

February 5th, 14th, 23rd
Guide Numbers: 6, 8, 4

Practical matters must be dealt with. Keep plugging and follow through on each task. Give yourself a pep talk to boost your self-confidence. There is nothing that cannot be overcome if you look at it in a positive light.

February 6th, 15th, 24th
Guide Numbers: 6, 8, 5

You have a lot of physical energy that needs to be released somehow. This is a good day to go on a short trip or play some sport you enjoy. You'd get restless staying home all day and would probably overeat.

February 7th, 16th, 25th
Guide Numbers: 6, 8, 6

Home, family and community affairs are highlighted; many demands will be made on your time and resources. An extra

The 6 Year: The Blossoming Time

responsibility could come your way. If you're in a position to give orders, avoid sounding dictatorial.

February 8th, 17th, 26th
Guide Numbers: 6, 8, 7

This is a good day to catch up on reading, writing or research projects. Your mental energy is high, and you should have no trouble thinking up clever ways of handling business and/or domestic matters.

February 9th, 18th, 27th
Guide Numbers: 6, 8, 8

Before you splurge on something, ask yourself if you really need it. Money is in focus and you may find yourself looking into different areas of investment or considering some major improvement for your home.

MARCH
Guide Numbers: 6, 9

Affairs of the heart (not necessarily your own) are highlighted this month. Loose ends are tied up and a situation that's been dragging on may come to a conclusion. This is an emotional time. Control your temper and guard against being resentful or possessive. Loved ones need your understanding.

March 1st, 10th, 19th, 28th
Guide Numbers: 6, 9, 1

You could find yourself volunteering for a project or deciding to improve your domestic situation. Before you jump into anything headfirst, make sure you weigh all the pros and cons and have a realistic course of action in mind.

March 2nd, 11th, 20th, 29th
Guide Numbers: 6, 9, 2

Affairs of the heart are highlighted: you are likely to feel more emotional than usual. Oversensitivity creates unnecessary problems. Try to keep things in perspective and be understanding of the needs of those close to you.

Your Daily Numerology

March 3rd, 12th, 21st, 30th
Guide Numbers: 6, 9, 3

You are likely to have difficulty with routine detail work and may wind up skipping over something important because your mind is elsewhere. If possible, schedule sedentary tasks for another day.

March 4th, 13th, 22nd, 31st
Guide Numbers: 6, 9, 4

Matters in the home are of prime concern. If you keep your goal in mind, whether it be new curtains or moving, the chores associated with it will seem to go faster. Let friends or family members assist you.

March 5th, 14th, 23rd
Guide Numbers: 6, 9, 5

You may find yourself in the midst of change—excited over the prospect of a new experience or reluctant to let go of something that has represented security. Try to remember that nothing lasts forever and remain adaptable in the face of new situations.

March 6th, 15th, 24th
Guide Numbers: 6, 9, 6

An important relationship may come to an end unless you are willing to make some adjustments. Try not to let feelings of jealousy, possessiveness or resentment gain the upper hand and avoid becoming emotionally involved in the affairs of others.

March 7th, 16th, 25th
Guide Numbers: 6, 9, 7

Your nerves are likely to be on edge, making you critical of yourself as well as others. Analyze the entire situation before jumping to conclusions—things may not be what they seem.

March 8th, 17th, 26th
Guide Numbers: 6, 9, 8

You are likely to be feeling organized and efficient and able to handle your own affairs quite nicely. However, take time out from your busy schedule for someone who needs your sympathy and understanding.

The 6 Year: The Blossoming Time

March 9th, 18th, 27th
Guide Numbers: 6, 9, 9
Today may bring a conclusion of some sort. You are likely to be feeling more emotional than usual and should guard against being possessive or intolerant.

APRIL
Guide Numbers: 6, 1
New ideas and a surge of energy get you off to a busy start this month. Go ahead with your plans, but first make sure you know what you want and that you are willing to face and accept the responsibilities that go along with it.

April 1st, 10th, 19th, 28th
Guide Numbers: 6, 1, 2
Someone may fail to live up to your expectations. Look carefully into both sides of an issue and listen to what others have to say. A compromise may be in order.

April 2nd, 11th, 20th, 29th
Guide Numbers: 6, 1, 3
A feeling of optimism prevails, and you are likely to be operating at full speed. Be careful not to do anything careless, such as stub your toe or knock your dinner off the stove by brushing a pot handle as you race to answer the phone.

April 3rd, 12th, 21st, 30th
Guide Numbers: 6, 1, 4
Duties and responsibilities keep you busy. Someone close to you may annoy you, but before you reprimand him or her, ask yourself whether you're expecting too much. Try to be sensitive to the feelings of others and to your own.

April 4th, 13th, 22nd
Guide Numbers: 6, 1, 5
An opportunity that seems too good to pass up may arise. However, take care not to bite off more than you can chew. Find some time for things that are important and don't let relatives interfere with your plans.

Your Daily Numerology

April 5th, 14th, 23rd
Guide Numbers: 6, 1, 6

Domestic concerns will keep you busy. You are likely to spend more time than usual in the kitchen, preparing for a large family dinner, community affair, or children's party. Take it easy and let others pitch in with a helping hand when it comes time to clean up.

April 6th, 15th, 24th
Guide Numbers: 6, 1, 7

This is a good day to delve into something that stimulates your mind, whether it be metaphysics or a good book. You'll probably feel like escaping into your own little world for a while, but don't neglect your responsibilities. Strive for material and spiritual balance.

April 7th, 16th, 25th
Guide Numbers: 6, 1, 8

You may be planning for others as well as yourself; those close to you could seek advice or support. Although there is no way to please everyone concerned, try to be as fair as you can when making decisions.

April 8th, 17th, 26th
Guide Numbers: 6, 1, 9

You may feel as though you are burning the candle at both ends when you try to juggle conflicting demands. You cannot handle everything at once; you may have to decide which aspects in your life are most important and eliminate some of the others.

April 9th, 18th, 27th
Guide Numbers: 6, 1, 1

This is a good day to start something new. However, if you are asked to make a commitment, be sure you know exactly what you're getting into before you accept. Don't take on more responsibilities than you can handle comfortably.

MAY
Guide Numbers: 6, 2

The 6 Year: The Blossoming Time

Patience, tact and a willingness to cooperate with others are this month's keynotes to success and happiness. Adjustments to those close to you are necessary; you'll achieve better results by clearing the air than by letting resentment build up. Try not to allow oversensitivity to lead you into making mountains out of molehills.

May 1st, 10th, 19th, 28th
Guide Numbers: 6, 2, 3

You are likely to be in a social mood. Sharing with others could give your spirits a boost; relationships should run smoothly if you are wise enough not to insist on having your own way all the time. Short visits or trips in the line of duty may take up a major portion of your day.

May 2nd, 11th, 20th, 29th
Guide Numbers: 6, 2, 4

Responsibilities may seem onerous, but self-discipline, resourcefulness and patience will see you through. Do what you can to avoid quarrels. Although it may not be apparent, your thoughtfulness is appreciated.

May 3rd, 12th, 21st, 30th
Guide Numbers: 6, 2, 5

You could find yourself doing something unexpected and family-related. Be tactful and patient, even if the situation is not exactly what you'd call fun.

May 4th, 13th, 22nd, 31st
Guide Numbers: 6, 2, 6

Family matters are likely to demand a great deal of your time; one person in particular may need your sympathy and understanding. Don't suffer in silence if you feel unappreciated or taken advantage of. It's better to clear the air by talking things out.

May 5th, 14th, 23rd
Guide Numbers: 6, 2, 7

You may feel as though there is a weight on your shoulders that you don't quite know how to handle. However, try to focus on positive thoughts and take things one step at a time. You can find comfort through the affection of someone close to you if you will only allow yourself to be approached.

May 6th, 15th, 24th
Guide Numbers: 6, 2, 8
Good judgment is very important: you may benefit from expert advice about some problem that's on your mind. A group activity that you help organize can be fun if you remain flexible and willing to give as well as take.

May 7th, 16th, 25th
Guide Numbers: 6, 2, 9
You may be feeling nostalgic when a celebration marks a conclusion of some kind. It could be a farewell luncheon for someone at work, a graduation dinner or a bon-voyage party for a friend. Savor your memories, but don't dwell on the past.

May 8th, 17th, 26th
Guide Numbers: 6, 2, 1
Although you may wish you could have it all to yourself, you will have to share something you value. It could be praise for an idea that was a joint effort, a prized possession or someone important's time, love or affection.

May 9th, 18th, 27th
Guide Numbers: 6, 2, 2
Detail work is highlighted. It's a good time to gather data, assimilate facts or consider alternatives before forging ahead on an idea. You could benefit from listening to the opinions of others and sharing your own time and talents.

JUNE
Guide Numbers: 6, 3
Friends and children are highlighted this month, along with your creative talents. All forms of self-expression are favored now, but take care not to gossip or be indiscrete. Entertaining is a source of pleasure; you may become interested in improving your

The 6 Year: The Blossoming Time

appearance or beautifying your home. Try not to spend extravagantly or spread yourself too thin.

June 1st, 10th, 19th, 28th
Guide Numbers: 6, 3, 4

Practical matters cannot be avoided, but creating order out of chaos is likely to give you a feeling of accomplishment. A pleasant interlude could be interspersed with your chores: you may celebrate someone's birthday at work with a cake, or a proud new father may hand you a cigar.

June 2nd, 11th, 20th, 29th
Guide Numbers: 6, 3, 5

If you are confined to routine chores and work, you may feel a bit restless. People contact is important; it would be a good time to go on a short trip or attend a game or social function. A romantic interest could grow or wane, depending on the substance of the relationship.

June 3rd, 12th, 21st, 30th
Guide Numbers: 6, 3, 6

A meal shared with friends or loved ones could be the highlight of your day, whether you play host or wind up being someone else's guest. Debts can be successfully collected if you go about things in a tactful way.

June 4th, 13th, 22nd
Guide Numbers: 6, 3, 7

This is a day to enjoy some solitude, if possible, and to choose your companions with care. Your mind is likely to be working overtime; interference from others will not be appreciated when you are absorbed in your thoughts.

June 5th, 14th, 23rd
Guide Numbers: 6, 3, 8

Business can be combined with pleasure, so it's important to put your best foot forward. Be conscious of how you manage your time, so as to avoid forgetting a commitment or arriving late for an appointment.

June 6th, 15th, 24th
Guide Numbers: 6, 3, 9

An expansive feeling of well-being could result when you help someone out, but don't neglect the needs of those close to you for someone who is a relative stranger. Your thoughts are likely to turn to romance, either real or fictitious.

June 7th, 16th, 25th
Guide Numbers: 6, 3, 1

You are likely to be feeling optimistic. A new beginning where an important relationship is concerned may be in focus, or you could be starting something new in your home. Energy should be high; this is a good time to act on any spark of creativity that pops into your mind.

June 8th, 17th, 26th
Guide Numbers: 6, 3, 2

A family matter could come up that will need your cooperation and understanding. Even happy occasions will require some tact and diplomacy on your part. Be careful not to take sides.

June 9th, 18th, 27th
Guide Numbers: 6, 3, 3

You may be more conscious than usual of how things look and have an urge to redecorate or purchase something for a loved one or for your home. However, take care not to be extravagant. A show or social event you attend with friends could be the highlight of your day.

JULY
Guide Numbers: 6, 4

Practicality is the keynote this month. It's a time for working hard and sticking to routine. There is much to be done and you may feel burdened by high expenses, responsibilities and the demands of others. You could also have to deal with a temporary change in your living conditions. Avoid being critical, resentful or giving unsolicited advice. The grass may seem greener elsewhere, but consider the matter from all sides.

The 6 Year: The Blossoming Time

July 1st, 10th, 19th, 28th
Guide Numbers: 6, 4, 5
    Responsibilities should not be neglected, even though unexpected activities are likely to break up your routine. There could be some change in your family or work situation, and you may have an expense in connection with a family matter.

July 2nd, 11th, 20th, 29th
Guide Numbers: 6, 4, 6
    This is a day for a family outing, but expect to be the one who makes most of the preparations. You may find you need to make many adjustments to the needs of others and could feel drained by the demands made on your time. Be realistic in your expectations or you may be in for a disappointment.

July 3rd, 12th, 21st, 30th
Guide Numbers: 6, 4, 7
    You are likely to be in for a trying experience, but make an effort to remain calm and collected. Even though you may feel annoyed or confused by the actions of others, do your best to smooth over a difficult situation without losing control.

July 4th, 13th, 22nd, 31st
Guide Numbers: 6, 4, 8
    Financial matters are highlighted: you may be concerned about an added expense. Home repairs could require your attention, or you may be faced with a medical bill. Be sure to use good judgment and efficiency in career and home alike.

July 5th, 14th, 23rd
Guide Numbers: 6, 4, 9
    You may be involved in an emotional matter not necessarily your own. Confusion in any area of your life is likely to irritate you—you will want to find out exactly where you stand.

July 6th, 15th, 24th
Guide Numbers: 6, 4, 1
    This is a day to take those steps that can make tomorrow better: perhaps make some change on your job, take care of home

repairs, get a physical checkup or settle problems in an important relationship. Progress should be in focus.

July 7th, 16th, 25th
Guide Numbers: 6, 4, 2
You will have many odds and ends to take care of and are likely to spend a good part of your time running errands and getting caught up on your chores. Try not to overlook any details. Diligence and conscientiousness pay off.

July 8th, 17th, 26th
Guide Numbers: 6, 4, 3
Although you may feel like doing something just for yourself, the day will not be entirely free of responsibilities. A short trip in the line of duty may be necessary. Take care not to indulge in capricious flirting—what you consider innocent fun could be misinterpreted.

July 9th, 18th, 27th
Guide Numbers: 6, 4, 4
Today's emphasis is on the home and practical affairs. Try not to be rigid or stubborn as you apply yourself to your tasks. Be realistic about the goals you set and don't take on more than your fair share.

AUGUST
Guide Numbers: 6, 5
This is an eventful month, bringing new concepts, travel and a touch of the unexpected. A legal matter may also require your attention. Contacts with people play an important role, and you may take a sudden interest in public affairs. Standing up for your beliefs is a necessity when criticism is directed your way.

August 1st, 10th, 19th, 28th
Guide Numbers: 6, 5, 6
Family and community affairs are highlighted; you could wind up with some additional responsibility before the day is

The 6 Year: The Blossoming Time

done. Take care not to say "yes" when you really mean "no" and don't feel guilty about asking for help.

August 2nd, 11th, 20th, 29th
Guide Numbers: 6, 5, 7
   You may be feeling touchy and irritable and should try to get off by yourself for awhile. Someone's nagging could get on your nerves or an upsetting remark could catch you off guard. Don't be unduly critical yourself and try to avoid jumping to conclusions.

August 3rd, 12th, 21st, 30th
Guide Numbers: 6, 5, 8
   You may have to muster up some extra strength to maintain control of a certain situation. Others could look to you for advice. Remember to use good judgment and keep your emotions under control.

August 4th, 13th, 22nd, 31st
Guide Numbers: 6, 5, 9
   Romance and adventure are in the air, making this a good day to go on a trip or expand your horizons. An unexpected conclusion could bring about a feeling of relief.

August 5th, 14th, 23rd
Guide Numbers: 6, 5, 1
   It's fine to do your own thing as long as you don't neglect your responsibilities. You're full of restless energy and should take special care to look before you leap. Something unexpected could come up that forces you to take a stand.

August 6th, 15th, 24th
Guide Numbers: 6, 5, 2
   You may have to deal with a minor disappointment or do something you don't relish. If you are bewildered by the behavior of someone close to you or feel you are being taken advantage of, make sure you bring matters out in the open rather than jump to conclusions.

August 7th, 16th, 25th
Guide Numbers: 6, 5, 3

You are likely to find yourself the center of attention sometime during the day. Social activities are highlighted, so if you want to have a party, this is an ideal time. However, don't be surprised if there are unexpected twists or turns.

August 8th, 17th, 26th
Guide Numbers: 6, 5, 4
The emphasis is on your home and family. You may be concerned about someone's health or a repair that requires your attention. Don't let an unexpected obstacle put you in a sour mood.

August 9th, 18th, 27th
Guide Numbers: 6, 5, 5
Don't be surprised if well-laid plans go unheeded when your schedule gets interrupted. An unexpected invitation may come your way. Be willing to experiment or take a chance. This is a good time to meet new people and try new things.

SEPTEMBER
Guide Numbers: 6, 6
Family and community are in focus this month, as well as a matter pertaining to health. Adjustment and compromise are necessary in order to maintain harmony in your environment. Circumstances may find you in a position to give advice, but avoid getting too involved. It is important that love and understanding pervade all your dealings with others.

September 1st, 10th, 19th, 28th
Guide Numbers: 6, 6, 7
Duties and responsibilities are likely to interfere with your need for some time to yourself. However, try not to be critical or fussy or play the role of martyr.

September 2nd, 11th, 20th, 29th
Guide Numbers: 6, 6, 8
Business and financial matters are highlighted. You could receive some unexpected income or be faced with a high expense.

The 6 Year: The Blossoming Time

Take care not to allow sentiment to interfere with good judgment should a family member require your help or advice.

September 3rd, 12th, 21st, 30th
Guide Numbers: 6, 6, 9

This is likely to be a busy day; you may find yourself sighing with relief at its end. Several activities (or one big one) may be planned, and you could be feeling more emotional than usual. Someone close to you needs your sympathy and understanding.

September 4th, 13th, 22nd
Guide Numbers: 6, 6, 1

Energy is high and you could find yourself taking on some new responsibility. Be careful not to take on too much and make sure you know exactly what you are getting into before you make a commitment.

September 5th, 14th, 23rd
Guide Numbers: 6, 6, 2

Associations with others are highlighted: a celebration could put you in a festive mood. You may have to make a compromise of some sort, but being cooperative and willing to share will bring its reward.

September 6th, 15th, 24th
Guide Numbers: 6, 6, 3

This is a good day for a family outing or for entertaining friends. However, responsibilities cannot be avoided entirely. A child or relative could require your special attention, or you may devote some time to beautifying your home.

September 7th, 16th, 25th
Guide Numbers: 6, 6, 4

Domestic matters will require your attention. Take your duties one step at a time, be organized and efficient. You will feel better once everything is in order and you are able to relax with a real sense of accomplishment at the end of the day.

September 8th, 17th, 26th
Guide Numbers: 6, 6, 5

Your Daily Numerology

The day could bring a change in your living conditions and possibly some unexpected news concerning a family member. You may be feeling restless and have trouble making yourself do the things you should be doing. Be sure you think before you act.

September 9th, 18th, 27th
Guide Numbers: 6, 6, 6
Home, family and community affairs are highlighted. Harmony or discord can result unless you are willing to accept responsibilities and make adjustments to those close to you. Restrain yourself from arguing unnecessarily or giving unwanted advice.

OCTOBER
Guide Numbers: 6, 7
You may be prone to periods of depression this month, but try to have faith and look on the bright side of things. Rest is important too. Take time out for mental pursuits and be willing to accept help if it comes your way. You are likely to spend more time alone, and there may be some matter you wish to keep secret.

October 1st, 10th, 19th, 28th
Guide Numbers: 6, 7, 8
Money is likely to be an issue: there could be some confusion over a bill. A decision that must be made could create some doubts or uncertainty in your mind. Don't be afraid to ask for advice.

October 2nd, 11th, 20th, 29th
Guide Numbers: 6, 7, 9
Differing points of view could have an adverse affect on a relationship, and nerves may become frayed as you try to free yourself from an undesirable situation. Straightforward conversation achieves better results than hot-headed arguments.

October 3rd, 12th, 21st, 30th
Guide Numbers: 6, 7, 1
New plans for living may begin to take form in your mind, but they could be accompanied by some fear and doubt. You may

The 6 Year: The Blossoming Time

find yourself embarking on a new path or having to face something on your own. This is a time to be self-sufficient rather than depend on others for help.

October 4th, 13th, 22nd, 31st
Guide Numbers: 6, 7, 2

You may be feeling misunderstood or taken advantage of. If so, honesty achieves better results than beating around the bush. Try clearing the air by talking things out rather than letting resentment build up.

October 5th, 14th, 23rd
Guide Numbers: 6, 7, 3

A social function may be highlighted; it's a good time to be with people you like. Words flow more freely, making it easier for you to express your ideas. But take care not to ramble or become involved in gossip.

October 6th, 15th, 24th
Guide Numbers: 6, 7, 4

Daily chores may seem burdensome, but if your surroundings are neat and orderly, you'll feel more comfortable and be able to concentrate more easily. The health of someone close to you could be of some concern.

October 7th, 16th, 25th
Guide Numbers: 6, 7, 5

Something important is likely to disrupt your routine or interfere with your plans. Try not to be hasty or take unnecessary risks. A hidden matter could come out into the open, causing some questions to be raised.

October 8th, 17th, 26th
Guide Numbers: 6, 7, 6

Duty is the keyword. Responsibilities cannot be overlooked, even though you might prefer to be doing something else. Try not to be too demanding or critical of those close to you and strive for harmony in your personal relationships.

October 9th, 18th, 27th
Guide Numbers: 6, 7, 7

Your Daily Numerology

You may feel torn between your own desires and those of loved ones. Overly critical people could make you irritable and touchy, and you may be in a critical mood yourself. Try not to be unrealistic in your expectations.

NOVEMBER
Guide Numbers: 6, 8

Business matters are highlighted this month, and you are likely to find yourself benefiting financially from some services rendered or from a property matter. Success depends on your being efficient, organized and able to hold your emotions in check. People in positions of influence may be of help to you; you could receive recognition for past efforts.

November 1st, 10th, 19th, 28th
Guide Numbers: 6, 8, 9

This is a good day to take care of a health, insurance or property matter. Think twice before pursuing a discussion on religion or politics; it could get heated.

November 2nd, 11th, 20th, 29th
Guide Numbers: 6, 8, 1

Business or financial matters could be on your mind, making you less sensitive than you should be to the feelings of family and friends. Although this is a good time to take the initiative and push for what you want, don't run roughshod over others.

November 3rd, 12th, 21st, 30th
Guide Numbers: 6, 8, 2

Some circumstances beyond your control could be a source of frustration, but try not to let it destroy your peace of mind. A delay that seems annoying is only temporary. Be willing to accept help from others.

November 4th, 13th, 22nd
Guide Numbers: 6, 8, 3

Communications are highlighted: you may find yourself discussing details with someone in a position of authority or giving a

The 6 Year: The Blossoming Time

report. Think before you speak, and make sure you choose your words wisely.

November 5th, 14th, 23rd
Guide Numbers: 6, 8, 4

This is a good day to do something to improve working conditions or a situation at home. Some problem or obstacle may need to be ironed out—work around it rather than fight it. Even though you may feel restricted or limited, don't become stubborn or headstrong.

November 6th, 15th, 24th
Guide Numbers: 6, 8, 5

This is a good day to promote yourself and your interests, but use good judgment in the process. You may find yourself having to make a quick decision. However, take care not to sacrifice future gains for temporary satisfaction.

November 7th, 16th, 25th
Guide Numbers: 6, 8, 6

Home, family and community affairs are highlighted; many demands could be made on your time and resources. Don't try to do everything yourself. Be willing to delegate some responsibilities to others.

November 8th, 17th, 26th
Guide Numbers: 6, 8, 7

Mental pursuits are highlighted; you could have an opportunity to learn something new. This is a good time to delve into a project that requires your concentration or to catch up on your correspondence. It's okay to analyze and perfect, but don't try to force any issues. Avoid committing yourself to something you may regret becoming involved in later.

November 9th, 18th, 27th
Guide Numbers: 6, 8, 8

Investments, home improvements and the needs of those close to you are highlighted. You may have an important decision to make regarding a business or financial matter. Think big, but be sure you are exercising good judgment before spending a great deal of money.

DECEMBER
Guide Numbers: 6, 9

This is a very emotional period. You may feel sad because an important part of your life comes to a conclusion or because you can't be with a loved one for a special occasion. Guard against self-pity; you have a lot to be thankful for.

December 1st, 10th, 19th, 28th
Guide Numbers: 6, 9, 1

You may find yourself burning the candle at both ends, and going back and forth from one person or project to another may exhaust you. It's fine to try to accomplish as much as you can, but try to recognize your limitations.

December 2nd, 11th, 20th, 29th
Guide Numbers: 6, 9, 2

This is a day to forgive and forget, to be generous with your time and love. You may be called upon to be a good listener or to work behind the scenes for a worthwhile cause. Sharing in someone else's joy or sorrow could be in focus.

December 3rd, 12th, 21st, 30th
Guide Numbers: 6, 9, 3

This is a good day to be seen and heard, but take care not to gossip or become indiscreet. Social interaction is highlighted: you may find yourself in the limelight at some point. A situation involving a friend or a child may be remembered for a long time to come.

December 4th, 13th, 22nd, 31st
Guide Numbers: 6, 9, 4

Responsibilities need to be shouldered: you could find yourself working hard for a cause. There may also be some change in your living conditions along with a lesson in self-discipline. Being realistic and willing to face facts can help overcome any obstacle in your path.

December 5th, 14th, 23rd
Guide Numbers: 6, 9, 5

The 6 Year: The Blossoming Time

You may be feeling some inner unrest and should take care not to be impatient with those close to you or to neglect your responsibilities. You could receive some unexpected news or a surprise visit from an old friend or relative.

December 6th, 15th, 24th
Guide Numbers: 6, 9, 6
Family and community responsibilities keep you busy, leaving little time for yourself. Take care not to impose your views on others. An effort to reform or change someone may prove disappointing, and a loved one may come to you for sympathy or advice.

December 7th, 16th, 25th
Guide Numbers: 6, 9, 7
Resentment and depression may be hard to avoid when you're faced with an upsetting situation, but you can find consolation in some spiritual or philosophical point of view. Be realistic in your expectations of others as well as yourself and avoid brooding over the past.

December 8th, 17th, 26th
Guide Numbers: 6, 9, 8
Decisions need to be made; a legal matter could require your attention. Although personal and business issues may get mixed up, don't let sentiment interfere with good judgment.

December 9th, 18th, 27th
Guide Numbers: 6, 9, 9
A completion of some sort may be difficult to adjust to at first, but the fact that the matter is settled should come as a relief. Try not to become so involved in some humanitarian effort or cause that you neglect the needs of those close to you.

CHAPTER EIGHT

THE 7 YEAR

"The Plants Bear Fruit"

GUIDE NUMBER: 7
COLOR: VIOLET

This is a year for solitude, introspection and intellectual pursuits. Analyze your goals and look for inner truths. Emotional conflicts need to be resolved. Withdraw from the rat race of superficial social activities—read, study and perfect your thinking. Take an ocean voyage, commune with nature, investigate the occult and develop a personal philosophy. You may not be feeling as energetic as usual, so rest is important to your well-being. You may also find yourself wanting to spend time alone and having a greater need than usual for privacy. Misunderstandings and disappointments could arise when those close to you object to your new ways of thinking and feeling, and a separation or broken friendship could result.

Success and happiness come through studying the deeper meanings of life. Materialistic pursuits should be avoided, as money will come your way only if it is not sought after. The less pushing, the greater the intake—and vice versa. Avoid neglecting your health, seeking escape, forcing issues, being critical or allowing unfounded inner fears and complexes to arise.

JANUARY
Guide Numbers: 7, 8

Your Daily Numerology

Business matters and material affairs come to the forefront this month; you may be doing some planning or managing for both yourself and others. Although money can be made, expenses are also likely to be high. Efficiency is the keynote to success. Try not to let your emotions interfere with common sense.

January 1st, 10th, 19th, 28th
Guide Numbers: 7, 8, 9

Your personal magnetism is high, and so long as you are realistic in your expectations, any social function planned for the day is likely to be a success. Try not to be rash or impulsive.

January 2nd, 11th, 20th, 29th
Guide Numbers: 7, 8, 1

This is a good day for handling banking or insurance matters. You may be feeling more energetic than you have for a while, but you could easily exhaust yourself if you undertake too much. Try to avoid a clash of wills with a male.

January 3rd, 12th, 21st, 30th
Guide Numbers: 7, 8, 2

Take care of important details at work. Co-workers will be willing to lend a hand if treated with tact and diplomacy. Try not to drag personal problems into other areas of your life.

January 4th, 13th, 22nd, 31st
Guide Numbers: 7, 8, 3

Communication skills are at a peak, so you should be able to get across what you want to say. Answer your mail, both business and personal.

January 5th, 14th, 23rd
Guide Numbers: 7, 8, 4

This is a day to get things done and work toward your goals. Try to be practical and realistic in all you do. A "poor-me" attitude may be hard to avoid when you feel limited or restricted in some way.

January 6th, 15th, 24th
Guide Numbers: 7, 8, 5

The 7 Year: The Plants Bear Fruit

An opportunity comes your way, but take care to exercise good judgment. Something that seems agreeable now may not prove wise in the long run.

January 7th, 16th, 25th
Guide Numbers: 7, 8, 6
You may feel like criticizing others. It's okay to express your opinions, but don't force them on anyone close to you. Try to make a loved one smile.

January 8th, 17th, 26th
Guide Numbers: 7, 8, 7
This is a good day for study and contemplation. It's unwise to skim over something just because it looks okay on the surface. Make sure you read the fine print before signing any papers.

January 9th, 18th, 27th
Guide Numbers: 7, 8, 8
Business and financial matters are highlighted; it's important to use good judgment in everything you do. Take care not to get involved in a power play. You may find yourself buying something that you would have considered beyond your budget not too long ago.

FEBRUARY
Guide Numbers: 7, 9
Completions of one kind or another are in the air: something is likely to come to an end, either through your own doing or through circumstances beyond your control. Try to let it go. This is not a good time to start anything new or be aggressive. Be tolerant and compassionate even when others annoy you.

February 1st, 10th, 19th, 28th
Guide Numbers: 7, 9, 1
Even though you may feel like being left alone to pursue your own interests, someone is likely to require your support. Try not to let inner unrest lead you to be hasty, impulsive or to bite off more than you can chew.

Your Daily Numerology

February 2nd, 11th, 20th, 29th
Guide Numbers: 7, 9, 2

You may be reluctant to express displeasure over something, but it would be better to bring matters out into the open than to let them smolder for hours. Others can't know how you feel unless you tell them.

February 3rd, 12th, 21st
Guide Numbers: 7, 9, 3

You are likely to see things through rose-colored glasses rather than as they really are. Get your errands over early and you can relax later. The spoken or written word is highlighted; you may receive news from a distance.

February 4th, 13th, 22nd
Guide Numbers: 7, 9, 4

Practical matters must be dealt with, and frustrations may seem to abound. However, if you have faith and a positive attitude, certain obstacles in your path will soon come to an end. Loved ones will appreciate a thoughtful gesture.

February 5th, 14th, 23rd
Guide Numbers: 7, 9, 5

Be adaptable to a change in plans. You could unexpectedly bump into an old friend or acquaintance. Be prepared to let go of something in a gracious manner.

February 6th, 15th, 24th
Guide Numbers: 7, 9, 6

Although you may feel that you're giving more than you're receiving, this is not the time to be concerned with yourself. Others need your understanding and compassion, and your good deeds will be rewarded a hundredfold if you don't look for an immediate return.

February 7th, 16th, 25th
Guide Numbers: 7, 9, 7

Spiritual and philosophical pursuits are favored; you may feel like going into seclusion for a while. Go on a retreat or take up some mind-expanding study. Something of a secretive nature could be a source of tension.

The 7 Year: The Plants Bear Fruit

February 8th, 17th, 26th
Guide Numbers: 7, 9, 8

This is a good day to take care of a bank or insurance matter. Think things out clearly and be sure you have all the facts before making any important decisions. Keep an open mind and try to avoid feeling resentful or intolerant of the views of others.

February 9th, 18th, 27th
Guide Numbers: 7, 9, 9

Say "good riddance" to a situation in your life that you no longer find satisfying and that has begun to drain you or make you miserable. All misunderstanding should be cleared up, so that nothing remains below the surface that may rise and trouble you later.

MARCH
Guide Numbers: 7, 1

New ways of thinking are highlighted this month. You may be feeling a surge of energy and a greater desire to be active, but try not to be unnecessarily forceful and don't allow yourself to become overly involved in the affairs of others. Mental and spiritual pursuits fare better than physical or material ones. Be open to learning new things.

March 1st, 10th, 19th, 28th
Guide Numbers: 7, 1, 2

You are highly sensitive and should avoid taking every comment personally or reading meanings into things that aren't really there. Jumping to conclusions could lead to false accusations or needless arguments.

March 2nd, 11th, 20th, 29th
Guide Numbers: 7, 1, 3

This is a social day, but you may encounter a situation that makes you wish you were somewhere else. It's a good time to write letters, go to the movies or pursue an artistic hobby. Don't talk too much about yourself or your plans for the future.

March 3rd, 12th, 21st, 30th
Guide Numbers: 7, 1, 4

Be constructive and attend to all those errands you've been putting off. However, it's a good idea to balance all this work with some rest and a sensible diet.

March 4th, 13th, 22nd, 31st
Guide Numbers: 7, 1, 5

You are likely to get bored with routine. Chores will go faster if you have something you can look forward to planned for later in the day. This is a good time to take a short trip or do something that's a little out of the ordinary for you.

March 5th, 14th, 23rd
Guide Numbers: 7, 1, 6

A family duty may crop up, and you may feel restricted in some way. However, once you've adjusted your schedule you will discover that things are not so bad after all. Being of service to a loved one has its own rewards.

March 6th, 15th, 24th
Guide Numbers: 7, 1, 7

Your physical energy is low; you would be better off pursuing mental or spiritual endeavors than indulging in intense physical activity. Beware of becoming emotionally involved with someone who's not available.

March 7th, 16th, 25th
Guide Numbers: 7, 1, 8

Your ability to solve problems and set things in order should be high, but try to avoid forcing issues. The more you push, the more obstacles are likely to appear. You may learn something about human nature before the day is out.

March 8th, 17th, 26th
Guide Numbers: 7, 1, 9

This is a time to forgive and forget and let go of the past. Loose ends have to be tied up before new ways of thinking and acting can take their place. Be open-minded and compassionate where others are concerned.

March 9th, 18th, 27th
Guide Numbers: 7, 1, 1

The 7 Year: The Plants Bear Fruit

Strive for inner peace. New ways of thinking are in focus: it is a good time for study or learning a subject you never gave much thought to before.

APRIL
Guide Numbers: 7, 2

Patience, tact and cooperation become necessary in your dealings with others. Things may not be all they seem this month. You would do well to look beneath the surface and pay attention to little details. An emotional matter is likely to give you food for thought, and an interesting contact could be helpful.

April 1st, 10th, 19th, 28th
Guide Numbers: 7, 2, 3

Don't believe everything you hear. Exaggerated or insincere statements should be taken with a grain of salt. Enjoy a social event for what it is and don't expect much in the way of deep conversation.

April 2nd, 11th, 20th, 29th
Guide Numbers: 7, 2, 4

You may feel that someone is being unduly critical, but don't let it put you in a bad mood. Practical matters need your attention; you should try not to let personal problems interfere with your work.

April 3rd, 12th, 21st, 30th
Guide Numbers: 7, 2, 5

Nothing seems to work out as planned, and unless you are adaptable to unexpected circumstances you could wind up feeling frustrated or even indisposed. Take time out for sensual pleasures: perhaps savor the taste of a favorite dish or enjoy the fragrance of a beautiful flower.

April 4th, 13th, 22nd
Guide Numbers: 7, 2, 6

Family activities are highlighted: you are likely to spend quite a bit of time with those nearest and dearest. Negative emotions may be hard to avoid when some fault-finding person touches a sensitive nerve. Try not to be fussy or critical yourself.

April 5th, 14th, 23rd
Guide Numbers: 7, 2, 7

Don't dismiss any of your first impressions. Your sensitivity is very high, making this a good day to follow your intuition. Be sure to get enough rest and take some time to be alone with your thoughts.

April 6th, 15th, 24th
Guide Numbers: 7, 2, 8

Something may come to the surface that you weren't aware of before. Or you could have a flash of perception that gives you insight into something you've always found bewildering. As you go forward with your plans for the day, take care not to disregard the feelings of relatives and friends.

April 7th, 16th, 25th
Guide Numbers: 7, 2, 9

Security could be an issue where your possessions or emotions are concerned. Do what you can to protect yourself, but don't let fear of the unknown hamper you from getting on with your life.

April 8th, 17th, 26th
Guide Numbers: 7, 2, 1

Although you may feel like forging ahead with your plans, this is not a good day to be pushy. It would benefit you to consider the wishes and sensitivities of others. Patience pays off.

April 9th, 18th, 27th
Guide Numbers: 7, 2, 2

You're likely to be feeling especially sensitive and may wish you had a shoulder to lean on. Since you are easily influenced by the moods of others, try to seek out the company of optimistic people.

MAY
Guide Numbers: 7, 3

The 7 Year: The Plants Bear Fruit

Romance is in the air this month. Social activities are a source of pleasure, and this is a good time to mingle with others, to express your thoughts and indulge in some creative outlet. Writing and artistic endeavors meet with especially favorable results. Don't let yourself get overemotional.

May 1st, 10th, 19th, 28th
Guide Numbers: 7, 3, 4

Try to find a happy medium between being lazy and working hard. Although you should not neglect anything that really needs to be done, this is not a time to overexert yourself. Problems should be brought out into the open; holding things inside could lead to a digestive upset or tension headache later on.

May 2nd, 11th, 20th, 29th
Guide Numbers: 7, 3, 5

If an appointment gets cancelled, find something else to do. Don't let a stubborn ego spoil your day and stand in the way of accepting a last-minute invitation. You could wind up having a wonderful time.

May 3rd, 12th, 21st, 30th
Guide Numbers: 7, 3, 6

Someone in your environment may make a decision you don't agree with. Before taking a defensive stance and becoming involved in a heated argument, try getting to the bottom of things and searching out all the facts.

May 4th, 13th, 22nd, 31st
Guide Numbers: 7, 3, 7

Things may not be what they seem, so don't go jumping to hasty conclusions. Emotions could be your worst enemy unless you find some creative outlet through which to express them. Writing down your thoughts is especially favorable.

May 5th, 14th, 23rd
Guide Numbers: 7, 3, 8

Money is likely to be an issue: deciding who pays for what when a payment is due, straightening out an incorrect bill, etc.

Try not to let your emotions rule your head. You can accomplish more by remaining calm.

May 6th, 15th, 24th
Guide Numbers: 7, 3, 9

Things may come to a head as you make up your mind to do away with some old aspect of your life. It may be throwing out that old tattered shirt or dropping out of an activity you no longer enjoy. Stick to your decision and don't look back. Your powers of persuasion are good and you should easily get your way.

May 7th, 16th, 25th
Guide Numbers: 7, 3, 1

Self-improvement may be on your mind, and you could decide to take up a new study or change the way you look. You may be feeling especially selective and put as much thought into what you buy as into choosing the company you keep.

May 8th, 17th, 26th
Guide Numbers: 7, 3, 2

If you can't be with loved ones, you are likely to spend more time than usual on the phone or writing letters to friends. Sharing your feelings with others is important.

May 9th, 18th, 27th
Guide Numbers: 7, 3, 3

This is a good time for socializing and you may enjoy the lively discussion that ensues when you go out with friends after a meeting or class. Music is likely to play a part in your day, whether it's listening to someone else's compositions or making your own.

JUNE
Guide Numbers: 7, 4

Practical matters need to be taken care of: you may feel the need to economize. Although your tasks must be performed thoroughly and conscientiously, try not to overdo things. Make sure you get enough rest and eat properly or your health could be affected. This is a good time to take a class or study something that could be of benefit to your career.

The 7 Year: The Plants Bear Fruit

June 1st, 10th, 19th, 28th
Guide Numbers: 7, 4, 5

You may have the opportunity to learn something new from an unexpected source. You could also feel disappointed by someone or something you have always liked before. Try to be adaptable to changes in your routine.

June 2nd, 11th, 20th, 29th
Guide Numbers: 7, 4, 6

Duties and responsibilities keep you busy; some compromise or adjustment will be necessary. Although you may have strong feelings about what is right or wrong, try to avoid bringing up subjects you know will start an argument or prompt an unpleasant response.

June 3rd, 12th, 21st, 30th
Guide Numbers: 7, 4, 7

Try to avoid crowds. Group activities may prove disappointing, and you could feel uncomfortable about some situation. A country outing or a long walk may prove uplifting.

June 4th, 13th, 22nd
Guide Numbers: 7, 4, 8

You can get a lot done if you put your mind to it, but leave nothing to chance. Analyze every situation carefully before making decisions. Although you may not see the results of your efforts immediately, you will see progress if you don't goof off.

June 5th, 14th, 23rd
Guide Numbers: 7, 4, 9

You could be feeling disappointed or sad. Try to keep busy with positive things so you don't have time to feel sorry for yourself. A stressful situation should be kept in proper perspective.

June 6th, 15th, 24th
Guide Numbers: 7, 4, 1

Preparing for the future may be on your mind. Only solid relationships will satisfy you, and you are likely to seek out the company of people who share your own interests.

June 7th, 16th, 25th
Guide Numbers: 7, 4, 2
You may be feeling overworked and underappreciated, but others won't know unless you tell them. If something is bothering you, discuss it tactfully with the person involved rather than let it fester inside. You'll feel better after getting things off your chest.

June 8th, 17th, 26th
Guide Numbers: 7, 4, 3
This can be a fun day provided you don't let negative emotions gain the upper hand. Try not to take things too seriously and let jealousy or possessiveness get you down. Creativity can be uplifting, and if you have any letters to write, this is the time to write them.

June 9th, 18th, 27th
Guide Numbers: 7, 4, 4
You may be feeling some pressure, from financial stress, a health matter or your job. Practical matters cannot be avoided; some uncomfortable fact may have to be faced. Spending time with optimistic people could help snap you out of a melancholy mood.

JULY
Guide Numbers: 7, 5
New interests and people are highlighted this month; someone long out of contact may reappear. Expect the unexpected. Although you may feel discontented with the status quo, avoid being hasty, impulsive or taking risks. Restless energy is best channeled into intellectual pursuits. A trip near or over water is a possibility.

July 1st, 10th, 19th, 28th
Guide Numbers: 7, 5, 6
You may feel torn between your own desires and those of loved ones. Responsibilities cannot be avoided—some situation is likely to be a source of tension. Try to be realistic in your expectations; if they are too high, you could be disappointed.

The 7 Year: The Plants Bear Fruit

July 2nd, 11th, 20th, 29th
Guide Numbers: 7, 5, 7

Lively and informative conversation will appeal to you, but you may find yourself irritated by small talk. Having your train of thought interrupted can be especially annoying.

July 3rd, 12th, 21st, 30th
Guide Numbers: 7, 5, 8

You may be feeling frustrated because you don't have enough control over a certain matter or because you want something you can't have. Good things come when you least expect them, but attempts to force issues can bring disappointment.

July 4th, 13th, 22nd, 31st
Guide Numbers: 7, 5, 9

This is likely to be a busy and eventful day with a touch of the unexpected. A live-and-let-live attitude will lessen frustration; you may have much to gain by keeping an open mind.

July 5th, 14th, 23rd
Guide Numbers: 7, 5, 1

Freedom to do your own thing will be important; any interference with your plans is likely to irritate you. Something new may come into your life, or you may have an unexpected experience that affects your way of thinking.

July 6th, 15th, 24th
Guide Numbers: 7, 5, 2

You could be feeling a bit blue for any of a number of reasons. Things may not happen as fast as you want them to or turn out the way you would like. Although the actions of others may upset you, you will do well to avoid an emotional outburst. Patience and tact are your best assets.

July 7th, 16th, 25th
Guide Numbers: 7, 5, 3

Your willpower may not be as strong as usual; frequent distractions could interfere with your getting things done. Take care not to be gullible or jump to hasty conclusions. Although a chance encounter may lead to romance, don't count on anything permanent.

July 8th, 17th, 26th
Guide Numbers: 7, 5, 4

Don't waste time procrastinating. A practical matter cannot be avoided and may require more of your time than you are willing to spare. Try to spend some time outdoors. Communing with nature could give your spirits a lift.

July 9th, 18th, 27th
Guide Numbers: 7, 5, 5

You may be full of restless energy; exploring something new could help alleviate a feeling of discontent. However, don't take any unnecessary risks—there's an unsteadiness around you. Plans may fall through, or someone you counted on may turn out to be unreliable.

AUGUST
Guide Numbers: 7, 6

Family matters, responsibilities and adjustments to those close to you are highlighted this month. Duty keeps you busy and you are likely to feel restricted in some way. Although obstacles can be frustrating, you could experience some happy moments through a younger person. Try to change worried thoughts into positive ones and snap yourself out of any depression you may get into.

August 1st, 10th, 19th, 28th
Guide Numbers: 7, 6, 7

You may feel like spending some time alone, but a duty or obligation could cause you to alter your plans. Try to avoid sarcastic or cutting remarks when someone fails to live up to your expectations or touches a sensitive nerve.

August 2nd, 11th, 20th, 29th
Guide Numbers: 7, 6, 8

Assuming more responsibilities than you can handle could lead to resentment, and you may feel burdened by those who depend on you. Delegate some of your duties to others rather than attempt to do everything yourself.

The 7 Year: The Plants Bear Fruit

August 3rd, 12th, 21st, 30th
Guide Numbers: 7, 6, 9

This is a good day to discharge a responsibility you've been putting off. Feel like cooking? Make dinner out of something you've had in the freezer for a long time. Try to avoid an argument with someone close to you.

August 4th, 13th, 22nd, 31st
Guide Numbers: 7, 6, 1

You could be feeling uneasy or discontented about something and may have to take on a leadership role or shoulder some added responsibility. Relationships could take a new direction.

August 5th, 14th, 23rd
Guide Numbers: 7, 6, 2

This is a good day for group activities—a gathering with family, friends or co-workers may be highlighted. Whether it brings pleasure or frustration could depend on your willingness to compromise and adjust.

August 6th, 15th, 24th
Guide Numbers: 7, 6, 3

Friends and children are highlighted; you could find yourself playing the role of host. Try not to take irritations too seriously. A sense of humor could help you be amused, rather than annoyed, by people's idiosyncrasies.

August 7th, 16th, 25th
Guide Numbers: 7, 6, 4

You are unlikely to have time to be frivolous. A general feeling of malaise could be coupled with resentment if someone proves untruthful or misleading. Try to see things from the other person's point of view and don't allow bitterness to fester.

August 8th, 17th, 26th
Guide Numbers: 7, 6, 5

Today could bring a sudden showdown; you may find yourself having to take a stand. Something unexpected that happens may not seem welcome at first but could turn out to be a blessing in disguise.

Your Daily Numerology

August 9th, 18th, 27th
Guide Numbers: 7, 6, 6

Duties and responsibilities are accented: you may be taking a trip in connection with a family or community matter. A health problem (not necessarily your own) could be a cause for some concern.

SEPTEMBER
Guide Numbers: 7, 7

Mental pursuits are highlighted this month; it's a good time to read, study or take a vacation. Pay attention to any flashes of intuition or psychic impressions that you may have. Do not try to force issues. Better results can be gained by letting things run their course. Make sure you get enough rest.

September 1st, 10th, 19th, 28th
Guide Numbers: 7, 7, 8

You may feel as though you're being manipulated, but try not to jump to hasty conclusions or let your emotions rule your head. You could be acting in a way that is demanding, critical or unrealistic. Progress can be made on an important project if you organize your time and efforts.

September 2nd, 11th, 20th, 29th
Guide Numbers: 7, 7, 9

Gaining wisdom and sharing it with others may be on your mind; you are likely to be concerned with intellectual or philosophical problems. You could bump into an old friend you haven't seen in a long time or could make a decision to leave someone or something behind.

September 3rd, 12th, 21st, 30th
Guide Numbers: 7, 7, 1

Mental and spiritual pursuits are highlighted, and you will not appreciate anyone who tries to divert you from your plans. You may find the pressure of others irritating and prefer to be alone, or you could experience a new way of thinking or decide to take up a study of some sort.

The 7 Year: The Plants Bear Fruit

September 4th, 13th, 22nd
Guide Numbers: 7, 7, 2
    Detail work is highlighted; you should take the time to do a job right rather than try to rush things along. Being alone or not having someone special by your side may result in melancholy feelings.

September 5th, 14th, 23rd
Guide Numbers: 7, 7, 3
    Although personal problems may be uppermost in your mind, try to keep them from being your major topic of conversation. This is a good day to enjoy the company of friends and to find some creative outlet for expressing your thoughts.

September 6th, 15th, 24th
Guide Numbers: 7, 7, 4
    Stick to schedules and associate with reliable, trustworthy people. Discipline yourself to get as much done as you can. Practical matters require your attention, and you could be feeling some pressure where finances are concerned.

September 7th, 16th, 25th
Guide Numbers: 7, 7, 5
    You may be experiencing a new sense of freedom but be a bit unsure of how to handle it. Someone's behavior could surprise you; you may discover something about human nature that you had never realized before.

September 8th, 17th, 26th
Guide Numbers: 7, 7, 6
    Certain responsibilities may interfere with your own needs, and you could get roped into an event you don't particularly want to attend. Try not to take on too much or you are likely to wind up irritable and resentful.

September 9th, 18th, 27th
Guide Numbers: 7, 7, 7
    You may be feeling apprehensive about something and could need some time alone to get hold of your thoughts and feelings.

Try not to brood or let unfounded fears get you down. Reading a book or listening to music could give your spirits a boost.

OCTOBER
Guide Numbers: 7, 8

Good judgment and organization are this month's keynotes to success and happiness. Business matters will occupy much of your time, but don't neglect someone close to you who expects your attention. There should be some relief where your financial affairs are concerned, and you may gain new insight into a matter that has been puzzling you for awhile.

October 1st, 10th, 19th, 28th
Guide Numbers: 7, 8, 9

This is a day to think before you act. Make sure you get expert advice and read the fine print before signing papers of any kind. A legal or health matter may require your attention, and you could receive some recognition for past efforts.

October 2nd, 11th, 20th, 29th
Guide Numbers: 7, 8, 1

Financial issues are likely to be on your mind; you may find yourself thinking about ways to save money or increase your income. A special occasion could be the highlight of your day.

October 3rd, 12th, 21st, 30th
Guide Numbers: 7, 8, 2

Do not neglect health or financial matters, no matter how insignificant they may seem. This is a time to take care of all those little details you might normally put off. Patience, tact and a willingness to cooperate will be needed in your dealings with others.

October 4th, 13th, 22nd, 31st
Guide Numbers: 7, 8, 3

Having someone to communicate with will be important to you, but give others a chance to get a word in edgewise. You may be in an extravagant mood and should take care to avoid impulsive spending which could be regretted later.

The 7 Year: The Plants Bear Fruit

October 5th, 14th, 23rd
Guide Numbers: 7, 8, 4
   You are likely to be more successful in perfecting older matters than in starting anything new. This is a good time to do your banking, make investments, deal with real estate or antiques. An unresolved problem may need to be taken care of, or you could experience some extra responsibility or expense.

October 6th, 15th, 24th
Guide Numbers: 7, 8, 5
   You may feel torn between two alternatives as "Should I or shouldn't I?" keeps going through your mind. Avoid making an impulsive decision, but take care not to vacillate so long that the opportunity disappears.

October 7th, 16th, 25th
Guide Numbers: 7, 8, 6
   Today's focus is on family and business associates. You may feel like telling others what to do, but keep in mind that their opinions could be as valid as your own. Some adjustment may have to be made due to a woman or a child.

October 8th, 17th, 26th
Guide Numbers: 7, 8, 7
   You may be feeling apprehensive about something. Try to get off by yourself for a while and think things over without getting emotional about them. Mental pursuits are favored; it's a good time to analyze and perfect your plans.

October 9th, 18th, 27th
Guide Numbers: 7, 8, 8
   A decision may have to be made concerning a business or financial matter. Power plays are likely. You may feel manipulated, or someone could resent your authority.

NOVEMBER
Guide Numbers: 7, 9
   Outside forces and circumstances beyond your control seem to be directing your life this month. As things change, courage

Your Daily Numerology

and conviction help you through an ending of some sort. Keep busy, show compassion for others and take nothing for granted.

November 1st, 10th, 19th, 28th
Guide Numbers: 7, 9, 1
   New plans could be taking form in your mind, but they may be accompanied by some doubts and fears. Concentrate on the future rather than waste time worrying about the past.

November 2nd, 11th, 20th, 29th
Guide Numbers: 7, 9, 2
   You may find yourself doing some soul-searching and wondering what's important in your life. The material things you've accumulated may not seem to mean much, and you could be feeling an emptiness inside.

November 3rd, 12th, 21st, 30th
Guide Numbers: 7, 9, 3
   You may be required to do some quick thinking when you are faced with a situation that requires an immediate decision or response. Take care not to be extravagant or spread yourself too thin. You may confuse or upset someone by your actions.

November 4th, 13th, 22nd
Guide Numbers: 7, 9, 4
   You could feel restricted or disappointed; an unpleasant fact may have to be faced. Try to concentrate on being positive and productive. You are likely to attract whatever you project.

November 5th, 14th, 23rd
Guide Numbers: 7, 9, 5
   Rivalry could be an issue. You may receive some unexpected news, but don't be gullible or ready to believe everything you hear. A change in plans that seems upsetting is likely to force you in a new and better direction.

November 6th, 15th, 24th
Guide Numbers: 7, 9, 6

The 7 Year: The Plants Bear Fruit

There could be an imbalance in a relationship: you may find yourself involved in domestic or family matters whether you like it or not. Do what you can to avoid misunderstandings and be willing to adjust and reconcile differences.

November 7th, 16th, 25th
Guide Numbers: 7, 9, 7
Unspoken words may be as important as those that are verbalized; something of a secretive nature could be a source of tension. This is a good time to take a trip or become involved in a mind-expanding study.

November 8th, 17th, 26th
Guide Numbers: 7, 9, 8
Something you've been waiting for may materialize or you could make a decision to bring a longstanding situation to an end. Money is likely to be on your mind, and a bank, insurance or real estate matter could require your attention. An expert's advice should be taken seriously.

November 9th, 18th, 27th
Guide Numbers: 7, 9, 9
You may be more temperamental than usual and could find yourself alternating between spurts of enthusiasm and uncertainty. Try not to let jealousy, possessiveness or resentfulness gain the upper hand. A personal relationship could flounder due to a misunderstanding.

DECEMBER
Guide Numbers: 7, 1
Action is the keynote this busy month, and you are likely to receive a welcome surge of energy. There is something you will have to do by yourself whether you want to or not. Although it is still best not to force issues, take advantage of opportunities that present themselves—especially where business matters are concerned. Good judgment is a must for future success. Financial affairs will show improvement.

Your Daily Numerology

December 1st, 10th, 19th, 28th
Guide Numbers: 7, 1, 2

Annoying details may cause the loss of valuable time; some compromise may be necessary in order to obtain what you want. Listen to what others have to say, but don't be gullible. This is a good time to collect facts or work on a hobby or collection.

December 2nd, 11th, 20th, 29th
Guide Numbers: 7, 1, 3

You could have some flashes of insight. Make sure you put your ideas down on paper so you don't forget them later. It may be hard to avoid feeling miffed when you fail to get the attention or appreciation you expect in a certain situation.

December 3rd, 12th, 21st, 30th
Guide Numbers: 7, 1, 4

This is a day to be practical and productive. Minor disappointments and delays may prove frustrating, but don't let them dampen your spirits. Accomplishing what you set out to do and getting chores out of the way will lead to a feeling of satisfaction.

December 4th, 13th, 22nd, 31st
Guide Numbers: 7, 1, 5

You may feel the grass is greener on the other side of the fence and find yourself wishing you could be somewhere else. However, avoid being hasty, impulsive or taking risks. Someone long out of contact may reappear in your life, or you could make a new friend.

December 5th, 14th, 23rd
Guide Numbers: 7, 1, 6

There could be some frustration connected with a responsibility. Although adjustments will need to be made, and you could find yourself doing some accommodating to those close to you, don't try to force your ideas on others or allow yourself to become more involved than necessary in their problems.

December 6th, 15th, 24th
Guide Numbers: 7, 1, 7

The 7 Year: The Plants Bear Fruit

You could unintentionally hurt someone's feelings unless you are willing to swallow your pride. Idle chit-chat is apt to frustrate you; you may want to cut short a visit with someone.

December 7th, 16th, 25th
Guide Numbers: 7, 1, 8

Energy and confidence are high. You may feel like getting out and accomplishing something, but the more you push, the less you gain where material matters are concerned. Try to avoid a clash of wills. Headstrong tactics bring disappointing results.

December 8th, 17th, 26th
Guide Numbers: 7, 1, 9

A feeling of frustration could result when something you were expecting does not materialize, or a new idea fails to work out as planned. A visit with someone you haven't seen in a while may be highlighted; reminders of the past could put you in a nostalgic mood.

December 9th, 18th, 27th
Guide Numbers: 7, 1, 1

You are likely to be absorbed in personal interests and endeavors and will resent anyone trying to divert your attention. A change in your thought patterns could result when you see something in a new light. Mental and spiritual pursuits fare better than physical or material ones.

CHAPTER NINE

THE 8 YEAR

"The Harvest Time"

GUIDE NUMBER: 8
COLORS: ROSE, GRAY, BLACK

This is a dynamic, materialistic year. Money may come from an unexpected source, but so could high expenses. There can be gain or loss, depending on how the other years in your cycle were handled. Business should prosper: it is an excellent time for buying and selling real estate. Your energy level is likely to be higher than it was last year, and you may suddenly have an urge to organize, whether it be kitchen cabinets or office personnel. Money is of prime concern; you are likely to feel ambitious and eager to improve your financial condition. This is a good time to invest, increase business activities, accept new challenges, direct others and overcome obstacles. But more than your bank account could expand—you could gain weight as well!

This is the year to push for the things you feel you deserve. Take command, ask for that raise or promotion, make things pay! Remember those seeds you planted in the 1 year? You'll reap the harvest now.

Success and happiness come through using good judgment, thinking big and being money-conscious, businesslike, efficient and practical. Avoid being greedy, unjust and letting your emotions rule your head. Although it is not a time for sentimentality, don't misuse your authority or treat others unfairly.

Your Daily Numerology

JANUARY
Guide Numbers: 8, 9

This is a busy and emotional period. You may feel confused or anxious about a decision that needs to be made and may have to let go of something you've grown accustomed to. A legal matter could require your attention. It is important to control your temper and not let your emotions interfere with good judgment.

January 1st, 10th, 19th, 28th
Guide Numbers: 8, 9, 1

You could have a brainstorm for making more money or improving your job. Think about it for a while, and if it's really feasible, plan to put it into action next month. A new romantic interest may be more appealing than an old familiar one.

January 2nd, 11th, 20th, 29th
Guide Numbers: 8, 9, 2

Try not to let your emotions rule your head. Details may annoy you, but they must be dealt with. Loose ends must be tied up before you can move on to something new. Have patience with a business associate who seems to ask inane questions.

January 3rd, 12th, 21st, 30th
Guide Numbers: 8, 9, 3

This is a good day for romance and socializing. Take time out to do something you enjoy—go to a concert or the theatre with a friend or paint a picture at home. You could hear from someone you haven't seen in a long time.

January 4th, 13th, 22nd, 31st
Guide Numbers: 8, 9, 4

Trying circumstances could annoy you; you are likely to feel limited or restricted in some way. Although certain chores may be unpleasant, you'll feel better when they're done.

January 5th, 14th, 23rd
Guide Numbers: 8, 9, 5

Unexpected problems in your personal relationships are likely to become a soure of frustration unless you adopt a "live-and-let-live" attitude. Give someone the benefit of the doubt.

The 8 Year: The Harvest Time

January 6th, 15th, 24th
Guide Numbers: 8, 9, 6
  Keeping harmony around you is important. Don't start or get involved in any needless arguments. Try to see things from the other point of view and be willing to compromise or make adjustments to the needs of a loved one.

January 7th, 16th, 25th
Guide Numbers: 8, 9, 7
  This is a good day to analyze and perfect your plans. Make sure everything is to your advantage and you know all the facts before taking action. It is important to read between the lines when handling business or financial transactions. A clear head now can avert emotional upset later.

January 8th, 17th, 26th
Guide Numbers: 8, 9, 8
  Organization and efficiency pay off. It's a good time to pay bills or get caught up on your paperwork. Financial matters are highlighted, but think twice before forging ahead with some business venture that you would be better off waiting until next month to start.

January 9th, 18th, 27th
Guide Numbers: 8, 9, 9
  A project or business matter may come to an end, leaving the way clear for you to start something new. Romance is indicated if you don't let a minor irritation spoil your day. This is not a good time to look for bargains.

FEBRUARY
Guide Numbers: 8, 1
  Action leads to success this month, especially where business matters are concerned, and an enticing offer may come your way. Be prepared to face things squarely and overcome obstacles that stand in your way. This is a time to use good judgment and forge ahead with your plans.

February 1st, 10th, 19th, 28th
Guide Numbers: 8, 1, 2

Your Daily Numerology

Use patience and tact in your undertakings. Don't put off taking care of details. It may be a good idea to seek expert advice about some matter that's bothering you.

February 2nd, 11th, 20th, 29th
Guide Numbers: 8, 1, 3

Accept social invitations that come your way. If you're in the market for a new romantic interest, you could attract one by being in the right place at the right time. A new person may help you make a difficult decision.

February 3rd, 12th, 21st
Guide Numbers: 8, 1, 4

Take care of practical matters, including your health. Although you may feel restricted in some way, organizaton and efficiency are a must. This is a time to plan and build.

February 4th, 13th, 22nd
Guide Numbers: 8, 1, 5

Your energy level is high and some physical outlet would be beneficial. Don't let an unexpected opportunity slip through your fingers. Be alert to recognize a good thing when you see it, whether it pertains to business or romance.

February 5th, 14th, 23rd
Guide Numbers: 8, 1, 6

New responsibilities come your way, but you should have confidence in your ability to meet their challenges successfully. What seems like hard work now could turn out to be a step toward a more rewarding career.

February 6th, 15th, 24th
Guide Numbers: 8, 1, 7

Mental pursuits are favored; your ability to analyze should be heightened. Take time out to be by yourself. You are likely to find interruptions more annoying than usual.

February 7th, 16th, 25th
Guide Numbers: 8, 1, 8

Business matters and financial dealings are highlighted. Constructive efforts in business and financial matters will meet with

The 8 Year: The Harvest Time

success. Don't let obstacles stand in your way. Take charge in an efficient manner.

February 8th, 17th, 26th
Guide Numbers: 8, 1, 9
You may find yourself sighing with relief as long-delayed matters finally come to a head. However, it's not quite time to let down your guard yet, New problems are likely to crop up and replace those just resolved.

February 9th, 18th, 27th
Guide Numbers: 8, 1, 1
This is a day to stick to your guns. Don't wait for someone else to solve your problems for you. Your numbers are favorable for moving ahead in whatever direction you chose. Take the initiative and act *now*.

MARCH
Guide Numbers: 8, 2
Patience and tact are this month's keynotes to success and happiness. You achieve the best results through being cooperative, accepting help from others and seeking expert advice. There is little you can do to speed things along, so attend to details without trying to force change. Although delays may be annoying, they are only temporary.

March 1st, 10th, 19th, 28th
Guide Numbers: 8, 2, 3
Interaction with others is highlighted; you are likely to be doing a lot of talking. It's a good time to entertain friends or to put your ideas across at work. If you have any speeches to make, be sure you have all the facts you need first.

March 2nd, 11th, 20th, 29th
Guide Numbers: 8, 2, 4
Your personal efficiency is high and you can accomplish a lot—especially in cooperation with a friend or co-worker. This is a time to cultivate solid relationships with people you can depend on and trust.

Your Daily Numerology

March 3rd, 12th, 21st, 30th
Guide Numbers: 8, 2, 5
    You are likely to be in for a surprise, possibly concerning a friend. A date may not turn out as planned, or you may suddenly see something in a new perspective.

March 4th, 13th, 22nd, 31st
Guide Numbers: 8, 2, 6
    This is a good day to give and take. Others may come to you for advice, but you may find yourself needing to consult an expert about an important decision. Work on a project goes better if you combine your efforts with those of someone else.

March 5th, 14th, 23rd
Guide Numbers: 8, 2, 7
    This is a good day for mental pursuits. If you have a project in mind, make an outline, figure out what materials you'll need and take care to choose the best person to help you get it done. Make sure your intentions are clear in both personal and business dealings.

March 6th, 15th, 24th
Guide Numbers: 8, 2, 8
    A good disposition may be as important as your executive ability. You can accomplish a lot more with the help of others than you can by yourself. Take problems in stride and be patient, even if you don't see results right away.

March 7th, 16th, 25th
Guide Numbers: 8, 2, 9
    This is a good day to tie up loose ends and get rid of annoyances, so that you can go on to new things. Try not to be jealous or possessive. Giving way to an emotional outburst could be regretted later.

March 8th, 17th, 26th
Guide Numbers: 8, 2, 1
    It's up to you to take the initiative, but you need other people's cooperation to get what you want. Patience and tact achieve better results than insisting on having your way. Be sure to show your appreciation to someone who does you a kindness.

The 8 Year: The Harvest Time

March 9th, 18th, 27th
Guide Numbers: 8, 2, 2
    This is a good day to be with others. Listen, observe and exchange ideas. Although delays may annoy you, there is little you can do to make things go faster. You may not feel as though you're getting much accomplished, but matters could look different in retrospect.

APRIL
Guide Numbers: 8, 3
    This is a month to do the things you enjoy—travel, entertain, add something wonderful to your wardrobe. Continue to use good judgment, however, and keep long-term goals in mind. Self-expression in any form is favored, and you are likely to be in an optimistic frame of mind. Your social calendar should be quite full; contacts you make now can be good for business as well as for your personal life.

April 1st, 10th, 19th, 28th
Guide Numbers: 8, 3, 4
    Some problem that needs to be faced and rectified could be brought to your attention. Concentrate on the tasks at hand. They may not be exciting (to say the least), but it's better to do them now than to put them off for another day.

April 2nd, 11th, 20th, 29th
Guide Numbers: 8, 3, 5
    Creative energy is high today, and you should have some free time to express it. Have fun, but guard against unnecessary extravagance or ostentation. Be adaptable to an unexpected change in plans.

April 3rd, 12th, 21st, 30th
Guide Numbers: 8, 3, 6
    Time will not be your own. Others require your attention—you may have to readjust your schedule to their needs. However, if you take care of your responsibilities you can have more time for yourself tomorrow.

Your Daily Numerology

April 4th, 13th, 22nd
Guide Numbers: 8, 3, 7
   Spend some time thinking about your future and how you can improve your financial situation. Make sure you visualize the whole picture as well as each part. If you have any doubts, get expert advice. Don't be careless or impatient.

April 5th, 14th, 23rd
Guide Numbers: 8, 3, 8
   This is a good day to organize something, whether it be a group activity or a car pool. Should you meet some opposition to your plans, deal with it in a calm and logical way. Try not to let your emotions get in the way of practical decision-making.

April 6th, 15th, 24th
Guide Numbers: 8, 3, 9
   You won't have time for everything you'd like to do, so channel your energies and talents into those activities you find most rewarding and worthwhile. Something to do with the performing or creative arts may be highlighted.

April 7th, 16th, 25th
Guide Numbers: 8, 3, 1
   You may have to take the bull by the horns if you want to get anything done. It's a time to use your own initiative rather than depend on others for help. Social contacts could be beneficial, but it's up to you to decide how.

April 8th, 17th, 26th
Guide Numbers: 8, 3, 2
   This is likely to be a busy day, with many details that need tending to. Friends will be helpful if you give them a chance; time will pass faster when you share your tasks.

April 9th, 18th, 27th
Guide Numbers: 8, 3, 3
   Do something to pamper yourself, but try not to spend more than you can afford if you decide to go on a shopping spree. A social invitation that comes your way could lead to a meeting with someone who will have a beneficial influence on your life.

MAY
Guide Numbers: 8, 4

Practical matters require your attention; your health may not be up to par. Although you feel burdened by work, try not to get discouraged. Keep plugging along and you'll come out ahead. If you are diligent and efficient, you will feel some relief by month's end.

May 1st, 10th, 19th, 28th
Guide Numbers: 8, 4, 5

You could be in for a work-connected surprise. A new project may come your way, one you're working on could suddenly change or you may meet someone you thought you'd never get to know. An unexpected expense could be a source of frustration.

May 2nd, 11th, 20th, 29th
Guide Numbers: 8, 4, 6

Something you've been working toward may materialize, or at least show signs of progress. Career and family responsibilities are heavy, and it will take all of the resourcefulness you can muster to fit in everything and everyone who demands your time.

May 3rd, 12th, 21st, 30th
Guide Numbers: 8, 4, 7

This is a good day to take up some study that could be beneficial to your career. Your mood will probably be serious, and idle chatter is likely to annoy you. Try to maintain a sense of humor.

May 4th, 13th, 22nd, 31st
Guide Numbers: 8, 4, 8

Even though this is a good day to exercise your leadership ability, try not to come across too strong. Be considerate of the feelings of others. Money could be an issue: you may be concerned about paying bills.

May 5th, 14th, 23rd
Guide Numbers: 8, 4, 9

A little misunderstanding may have to be cleared up—perhaps a rumor or some gossip that got to the wrong person. Loose ends need to be taken care of in order to make way for new activities.

Your Daily Numerology

May 6th, 15th, 24th
Guide Numbers: 8, 4, 1

Energy and confidence are high; you should be in control of all your affairs. Just make sure you are channeling your energies in the right direction. Your future financial security could depend on your making wise decisions.

May 7th, 16th, 25th
Guide Numbers: 8, 4, 2

Things could happen in doubles—two party invitations, two doctor's appointments or two kids soliciting at the door. Be careful you don't make two dates for the same night! Although many little details require your attention, try not to let petty annoyances rattle you.

May 8th, 17th, 26th
Guide Numbers: 8, 4, 3

This is a good day to mix business with pleasure. A lively discussion with co-workers over lunch could lead to a sudden insight about the difficulty with a project you've been working on. If you're single, someone at your office could introduce you to a new romantic prospect.

May 9th, 18th, 27th
Guide Numbers: 8, 4, 4

Solid relationships are an issue; you are unlikely to put up with unreliability or vacillation about making a commitment. It's time to face facts and work toward getting results. Organize your affairs and don't waste time.

JUNE
Guide Numbers: 8, 5

Change and a greater amount of personal freedom color this active month. New interests lead to new ideas; a short trip is likely. Being on the alert could lead to unexpected gain through contacts with other people. However, take care to be businesslike and courteous with associates even if they annoy you.

June 1st, 10th, 19th, 28th
Guide Numbers: 8, 5, 6

The 8 Year: The Harvest Time

A club function or community project could demand your attention. Using your talents to help others is not only satisfying but can be beneficial to your social life.

June 2nd, 11th, 20th, 29th
Guide Numbers: 8, 5, 7
Underneath a friendly facade you may be feeling a bit low. Try not to brood or be oversensitive; find a few minutes to be by yourself and think things out in an unemotional way.

June 3rd, 12th, 21st, 30th
Guide Numbers: 8, 5, 8
You will have to make a decision regarding a personal, business or real estate matter. A lump sum of money may come your way, but you could also encounter some unexpected frustration through a high expense. Take care not to break something of value.

June 4th, 13th, 22nd
Guide Numbers: 8, 5, 9
This is a good day to broaden the scope of your interests. You may find yourself engaged in some educational pursuit of a career-oriented or philosophical nature. Plans are subject to change or cancellation; you may suddenly decide you no longer need something you once thought necessary.

June 5th, 14th, 23rd
Guide Numbers: 8, 5, 1
Curiosity and energy are high. You may find yourself embarking on a new venture or project, or a new opportunity may come your way. Make sure you use good judgment before taking action of any kind.

June 6th, 15th, 24th
Guide Numbers: 8, 5, 2
You may be prone to oversensitivity and could get rattled over little things that crop up unexpectedly. Patience, good judgment and a willingness to cooperate are your best assets. Try to work *with* others rather than against them.

June 7th, 16th, 25th
Guide Numbers: 8, 5, 3

Your Daily Numerology

You are likely to be in a gregarious mood, but make sure you exercise good judgment and are discreet in your dealings with others. Avoid gossip of any kind and don't believe everything you hear. You may be doing some traveling (not necessarily of a long-distance nature).

June 8th, 17th, 26th
Guide Numbers: 8, 5, 4

Some problem may need to be ironed out. Don't fritter away your time on frivolous activities. Make an effort to clear away obstacles in your path and try to keep a clear head. Frayed nerves could lead to a digestive upset.

June 9th, 18th, 27th
Guide Numbers: 8, 5, 5

Try not to become involved with too many things at once. An unexpected brainstorm or opportunity may result in improved conditions if followed up, but scattering your energies in too many directions could be self-defeating.

JULY
Guide Numbers: 8, 6

Adjustments have to be made to family and business associates this month; the illness of someone close to you could create extra responsibilities or expenses. Although you may feel burdened by the needs of others, try to remain patient and sympathetic. Strive for harmony in your surroundings. Those who are single may find romance.

July 1st, 10th, 19th, 28th
Guide Numbers: 8, 6, 7

Domestic or community responsibilities could interfere with your career, leaving you physically and emotionally drained. Try to take things in stride, even though those close to you may prove irritating. Avoid excessive worry and get some rest.

July 2nd, 11th, 20th, 29th
Guide Numbers: 8, 6, 8

The 8 Year: The Harvest Time

You may find yourself in a competitive situation or having to defend your position on some issue. Good judgment and efficiency pay off: time spent making schedules or organizing your affairs will not be wasted. An added business or family expense could come up.

July 3rd, 12th, 21st, 30th
Guide Numbers: 8, 6, 9
This is a day to forgive, forget and let go of the past. The end of one situation could mark the beginning of something better. Take care not to let an emotionally tense situation lead to an outburst of temper.

July 4th, 13th, 22nd, 31st
Guide Numbers: 8, 6, 1
A family or work situation may require your attention. You could find yourself volunteering for a community project or being elected to an office of some sort. Meeting new responsibilities can be rewarding and lead to a sense of accomplishment.

July 5th, 14th, 23rd
Guide Numbers: 8, 6, 2
Sharing with others is highlighted; this is a good time for a family or company outing. A compromise may be necessary in order to get what you want. Be willing to cooperate and listen to what others have to say.

July 6th, 15th, 24th
Guide Numbers: 8, 6, 3
Communications are highlighted, but try to keep gossip down to a minimum. Betraying a confidence could lead to regrets later. Make an effort to keep your mind on what you are doing or distractions could create problems.

July 7th, 16th, 25th
Guide Numbers: 8, 6, 4
Today's emphasis is on those close to you—friends, family, co-workers. There could be some discord or frustration on your job. Be organized and efficient in whatever you do and try not to forget anything important.

Your Daily Numerology

July 8th, 17th, 26th
Guide Numbers: 8, 6, 5

Some change in plans or disruption in your routine may be in store for you. Make sure you exercise good judgment before taking a chance where you would ordinarily be cautious.

July 9th, 18th, 27th
Guide Numbers: 8, 6, 6

The emphasis is on responsibilities and relationships: you could find yourself involved in some group or community activity. You may feel that certain people are being too demanding of your time, but afterward you'll probably be glad to have had their company.

AUGUST
Guide Numbers: 8, 7

An overactive imagination could lead to loneliness, apprehension and the blues. However, these feelings are likely to be entirely of your own making. You may need some time to think things out and could benefit from a relaxing vacation in a quiet spot. Have faith, and by month's end you will find that your affairs are in better shape than you first thought.

August 1st, 10th, 19th, 28th
Guide Numbers: 8, 7, 8

Even though your schedule is likely to be heavy, try not to be too serious or intense. Time out for rest is also important. You may find yourself doing some organizing or planning behind the scenes.

August 2nd, 11th, 20th, 29th
Guide Numbers: 8, 7, 9

Unfinished business may be the subject of discussion, but it is still likely to linger on for a while. However, once you put the past behind you, new channels will open up. This is a good time to get together with an old friend.

August 3rd, 12th, 21st, 30th
Guide Numbers: 8, 7, 1

The 8 Year: The Harvest Time

Although business and personal interests may be moving along, don't expect to see the full results of your efforts yet. Avoid being overanxious or pushy. Something you experience may help you distinguish a true friend from one of the fair-weather kind.

August 4th, 13th, 22nd, 31st
Guide Numbers: 8, 7, 2

You may be feeling a bit low and have a need to discuss something that's bothering you. Interaction with others could be a comfort. Try to take care of details as they arise and organize your time and efforts as well as you can.

August 5th, 14th, 23rd
Guide Numbers: 8, 7, 3

This is a good day for communication of any kind. Your ability to express yourself is high and you shouldn't have any trouble getting your point across. A situation that seems appealing on the surface may have a string attached.

August 6th, 15th, 24th
Guide Numbers: 8, 7, 4

Practical affairs need to be taken care of and may demand more of your time than you would like. Although it is important to get as much accomplished as you can, try not to overdo things.

August 7th, 16th, 25th
Guide Numbers: 8, 7, 5

Something unexpected could make this a day to remember —a hidden fact may come to light or a business matter or relationship could take a new direction. Don't throw away something you may be able to use later.

August 8th, 17th, 26th
Guide Numbers: 8, 7, 6

A willingness to compromise and make adjustments can produce some surprising results. Strive for harmony in your surroundings and try not to let misunderstandings or domestic hassles get you down. Avoid being critical of those close to you.

August 9th, 18th, 27th
Guide Numbers: 8, 7, 7

Your Daily Numerology

This is a day to think and plan. Avoid acting hastily or making impulsive decisions. Social events, unless they involve your closest friends, would be best put off for another day.

SEPTEMBER
Guide Numbers: 8, 8

Good judgment is important this month. It is a time to push for what you want, and expert advice can help prevent mistakes. Don't take a back seat when you should act on some issue. You may be determined to rid yourself of a difficult situation which has been disturbing your peace of mind, but avoid being headstrong or resentful.

September 1st, 10th, 19th, 28th
Guide Numbers: 8, 8, 9

You may find yourself in the midst of some sort of transition. A project or relationship could reach its conclusion or you might find yourself dealing with a separation (not necessarily a permanent one). Be philosophical and accept others for what they are.

September 2nd, 11th, 20th, 29th
Guide Numbers: 8, 8, 1

You can take strides toward improving your financial situation. Be forceful and aggressive if you must, but avoid being greedy or insensitive. New ideas may influence your plans and you could find yourself reorganizing something in a different way.

September 3rd, 12th, 21st, 30th
Guide Numbers: 8, 8, 2

Meetings, associations with others and conferences are all highlighted. Although you may find yourself immersed in minor tribulations, try to keep long-term goals in mind. A friend or loved one may be influential in your spending.

September 4th, 13th, 22nd
Guide Numbers: 8, 8, 3

You'll probably feel like enjoying the finer things of life and may be in an extravagant mood. Take care not to overspend. First impressions may be important, so make sure you look your best.

The 8 Year: The Harvest Time

September 5th, 14th, 23rd
Guide Numbers: 8, 8, 4
    You'll be concerned with practical matters; a high expense could be a source of frustration. Although you may feel you haven't enough time, you can get a lot accomplished if you are organized and efficient.

September 6th, 15th, 24th
Guide Numbers: 8, 8, 5
    People contact is highlighted; scattered thoughts may make it difficult for you to keep your mind on one thing. A good sense of direction could be a blessing. If you're in doubt, ask someone to show you the way.

September 7th, 16th, 25th
Guide Numbers: 8, 8, 6
    Responsibilities cannot be ignored. Someone may need your help or advice, or you could become involved in a community project. Try to avoid being judgmental. Seek to establish harmony in your surroundings and reconcile conflicts with an open mind.

September 8th, 17th, 26th
Guide Numbers: 8, 8, 7
    You may find yourself indulging in flights of fantasy and have to force yourself to use self-discipline if you want to get everything done that you should. Time out for some quiet pursuit or a long walk could leave you refreshed and relaxed.

September 9th, 18th, 27th
Guide Numbers: 8, 8, 8
    Today's focus is on financial matters: money could come in or go out. An investment may require attention. It is important to use good judgment and to be fair in all your dealings with others.

OCTOBER
Guide Numbers: 8, 9
    Compassion and forgiveness are the keynotes to success and happiness this month. Emotional stress may start to build, so you must guard against lashing out at someone. Try to settle your

differences without being hurtful or offensive. You may want to clean closets or otherwise get rid of things that have outlived their usefulness. A relationship or situation you've been involved in could come to an end.

October 1st, 10th, 19th, 28th
Guide Numbers: 8, 9, 1

You may feel as though you are in a period of transition and be anxious for a change. However take care not to be hasty. Good judgment is still a must, and you should be aware of the consequences of any decisions you might make.

October 2nd, 11th, 20th, 29th
Guide Numbers: 8, 9, 2

Little things can get on your nerves; your patience is likely to be tested. Try to be understanding of others who are slower than you or who fail to give you the support you expected. You may find yourself sharing some knowledge or skill.

October 3rd, 12th, 21st, 30th
Guide Numbers: 8, 9, 3

The limelight is likely to be yours—at least for a while. Try not to get carried away by your emotions, however, or let touchiness get the best of you. You could hear some news that will affect your future or that of someone close to you.

October 4th, 13th, 22nd, 31st
Guide Numbers: 8, 9, 4

You may feel discouraged by some limitation or obstacle. Try to maintain a sense of humor and see things in a positive light. Perseverance and determination pay off, and the better organized you are the more you can achieve.

October 5th, 14th, 23rd
Guide Numbers: 8, 9, 5

This is a day to be adaptable to last-minute surprises. Something unexpected may cause you to break your routine, or there could be a change in plans. Don't jump to conclusions about someone whose actions annoy you. Make sure you have all the facts first and count to ten before blowing your cool.

The 8 Year: The Harvest Time

October 6th, 15th, 24th
Guide Numbers: 8, 9, 6

Those close to you may require your sympathy and understanding. Try not to be short-tempered with someone who doesn't do things your way. There could be more than one right answer; his or her opinion may be just as valid as your own.

October 7th, 16th, 25th
Guide Numbers: 8, 9, 7

You may be feeling mentally weary or depressed and could benefit from some time alone. Dealing with red tape or bureaucracy is apt to irritate you. Be willing to accept assistance if it comes your way, even though it may not be from the person you would prefer.

October 8th, 17th, 26th
Guide Numbers: 8, 9, 8

You will feel more in control if you have things organized in your personal life as well as in your career. This is a day to be practical and efficient. However, try not to be oblivious to others or you could unintentionally hurt someone's feelings.

October 9th, 18th, 27th
Guide Numbers: 8, 9, 9

A business matter or project may reach its conclusion, or you could be thinking about getting rid of something that has outlived its usefulness. Try not to let your emotions rule your head. Careless spending of money or time is likely to lead to regret.

NOVEMBER
Guide Numbers: 8, 1

Action is the keynote for success and happiness this month. However, taking care of health matters is also important. This is a good time to get yourself checked out. Business affairs are favorably highlighted and new beginnings are likely in these areas. A property or insurance matter may also require your attention.

November 1st, 10th, 19th, 28th
Guide Numbers: 8, 1, 2

Patience, tact and diplomacy will be required in your dealings with others. Even though you may feel like forging ahead on your own, you will need their cooperation to accomplish your goals.

November 2nd, 11th, 20th, 29th
Guide Numbers: 8, 1, 3
　　The day could see the birth of a creative idea or venture, or you may decide to get back to work on a talent that has been neglected for a while. Make sure you look your best at all times and get out and circulate. An opportunity could come through a friend or a social event.

November 3rd, 12th, 21st, 30th
Guide Numbers: 8, 1, 4
　　Concern about your security may prompt you to take steps to improve your financial status or a relationship. This is a good time to eliminate bad habits and substitute beneficial ones. Obstacles *can* be overcome if you organize your time and efforts realistically.

November 4th, 13th, 22nd
Guide Numbers: 8, 1, 5
　　A variety of people may cross your path, triggering new ideas or interests that open up some avenue you hadn't considered before. Be prepared for surprises. Change may occur quickly and when you least expect it.

November 5th, 14th, 23rd
Guide Numbers: 8, 1, 6
　　You may be presented with a new problem or find yourself having to take charge of some situation. Duty and adjustment are the keywords, and whether you find others helpful or upsetting will depend largely on your attitude and point of view.

November 6th, 15th, 24th
Guide Numbers: 8, 1, 7
　　You may be feeling drained; some time alone could come as a relief. Although you prefer working by yourself and remaining behind the scenes, try not to be too critical of those who offer their help.

The 8 Year: The Harvest Time

November 7th, 16th, 25th
Guide Numbers: 8, 1, 8
   This is a day to be productive and organize your time so that you can get as much done as possible. Money matters may be on your mind: you could make a decision to improve your financial situation in some way.

November 8th, 17th, 26th
Guide Numbers: 8, 1, 9
   A situation may come to an end, either through your own doing or through circumstances beyond your control. Although you could be feeling angry or sad or even left out, it is important to remember that endings are necessary to clear the way for new beginnings.

November 9th, 18th, 27th
Guide Numbers: 8, 1, 1
   This is a day to stand on your own two feet and do what *you* think is right. Energy and confidence are high; you may find yourself in a leadership role, whether chairing a meeting or giving advice. However, avoid being arrogant or insensitive.

DECEMBER
Guide Numbers: 8, 2
   Details that need to be taken care of and duties that must be assumed could seem overwhelming this month. But even though you may feel somewhat tired and confused, you are not alone. Someone is willing to help out if only you give him or her the chance. A person or situation will need your understanding.

December 1st, 10th, 19th, 28th
Guide Numbers: 8, 2, 3
   This is a day to think before you speak. Words can backfire if you say too much to the wrong people. You could encounter many distractions and should take care not to let them interfere with your duties.

December 2nd, 11th, 20th, 29th
Guide Numbers: 8, 2, 4

Your Daily Numerology

Productive work and stable relationships will give you a feeling of satisfaction, but you are likely to be hurt or disappointed if someone you counted on proves unreliable. Try to stick to a sensible routine and refuse to let others confuse you with their demands.

December 3rd, 12th, 21st, 30th
Guide Numbers: 8, 2, 5

Small annoyances or surprises may be the order of the day; something is likely to turn out quite differently than you had planned. You could bump into an old friend or be in touch with someone you haven't heard from for a while.

December 4th, 13th, 22nd, 31st
Guide Numbers: 8, 2, 6

You may be called upon to be a good listener. Sharing a situation or a common goal is likely to give you a feeling of satisfaction, but try not to get emotionally involved in the problems of others.

December 5th, 14th, 23rd
Guide Numbers: 8, 2, 7

You may be feeling more sensitive than usual and little things could bother you that are ordinarily easily taken in stride. All may not be what it seems, so take care not to jump to conclusions or read more into a situation than is really there.

December 6th, 15th, 24th
Guide Numbers: 8, 2, 8

You will need to be both efficient and cooperative. It will behoove you to remain on the alert and attentive to what others have to say. Cash in on something you have been holding for a rainy day or invest in a collector's item.

December 7th, 16th, 25th
Guide Numbers: 8, 2, 9

Finish up last-minute details so you don't have to concern yourself with them later on. This is a good time for sharing with others, whether it be your thoughts, a skill or a contribution to your favorite charity. A trip may fail to materialize as planned.

The 8 Year: The Harvest Time

December 8th, 17th, 26th
Guide Numbers: 8, 2, 1

This is a day to take the initiative, but it is also important to be cooperative and considerate as well. Although something may seem to take much longer than you think it should, getting upset won't help matters.

December 9th, 18th, 27th
Guide Numbers: 8, 2, 2

You may have to meet with someone to discuss details, but don't try to force any issues. This is a time to accept the help of others and listen to expert advice. You are especially susceptible to changes in your environment and little things can affect your mood.

CHAPTER TEN

THE 9 YEAR

"Time to Clean Up After the Harvest and Get Ready for the New Planting Year."

GUIDE NUMBER: 9
COLORS: ALL COLORS, ESPECIALLY REDDISH GOLD and AUTUMN TONES

This is a cleansing year between the end of one cycle and the beginning of the next, and with it comes a loss or ending of some kind. It is a time to let go of relationships that have been outgrown or to get rid of the outmoded in order to make way for the new and worthwhile. Don't be surprised if your fancies suddenly turn to sorting things out, cleaning closets or giving away clothes that haven't been worn in years. You may feel nostalgic and even a little sad at having to let go of some things, but it's a necessity. Your emotions are very vulnerable and your temper is easily sparked.

Although this is not a good year to start anything new, it does favor writing, acting, publishing, learning, teaching others or donating your time and money to a worthwhile cause. Complete your projects, finish things up and take a long trip if you so desire.

Success and happiness come through compassion, humanitarian efforts, being emotionally detached and letting go of whatever starts to leave your life. Avoid being indiscrete, jealous, selfish, possessive or overly emotional in any way.

JANUARY
Guide Numbers: 9, 1

New plans for living could be forming in your mind as some sort of beginning or a change in outlook takes place. You may experience some uncertainty as well. Don't depend on others to do things you should be taking care of yourself.

January 1st, 10th, 19th, 28th
Guide Numbers: 9, 1, 2

Play your hunches where romance is concerned, but listen to the advice of others when dealing with a financial matter. Try not to be overly sensitive. A comment intended as constructive criticism may bother you more than it should.

January 2nd, 11th, 20th, 29th
Guide Numbers: 9, 1, 3

This is a good day to go out and have some fun. All forms of self-expression and creativity are favored; you'll find it difficult to keep your mind on anything of a practical nature. A new friendship could lead to romance, but don't count on it becoming permanent.

January 3rd, 12th, 21st, 30th
Guide Numbers: 9, 1, 4

Get your home or work area in order, whether you clean out the refrigerator or just sort through clutter that's been accumulating for a while. You should have more than enough energy to do whatever needs to be done.

January 4th, 13th, 22nd, 31st
Guide Numbers: 9, 1, 5

Unexpected twists and turns test your adaptability and resourcefulness. Don't cling to old ideas or antiquated ways of doing things. It's fine to go out on the town tonight, but try not to overindulge.

January 5th, 14th, 23rd
Guide Numbers: 9, 1, 6

The 9 Year: Clean Up

You may find yourself offering to be of service. However, it could be something as simple as offering an aspirin or being willing to lend a sympathetic ear. Much can be accomplished if you don't waste energy worrying about things over which you have no control.

January 6th, 15th, 24th
Guide Numbers: 9, 1, 7

This is a good day to examine your philosophy of life. If there is anything you would like to change, focus on the steps you can take to change it. Spend as much time as you can by yourself and make sure you get enough rest.

January 7th, 16th, 25th
Guide Numbers: 9, 1, 8

Good judgment pays off: you could cash in on something you've been holding on to for a while. Don't let feelings of jealousy or possessiveness gain the upper hand—you must be willing to let go of the old in order to make room for the new.

January 8th, 17th, 26th
Guide Numbers: 9, 1, 9

You could have an urge to be done with certain things, but take care not to act on impulse alone. This is likely to be an emotional time, and you may be more temperamental than usual.

January 9th, 18th, 27th
Guide Numbers: 9, 1, 1

Spurts of creative energy influence you and you are likely to embark on a new project or venture. Don't let doubts or feelings of uncertainty dampen your spirit. Someone may be depending on your strength and guidance.

FEBRUARY
Guide Numbers: 9, 2

Oversensitivity could be a stumbling block this month. Try to keep your emotions in check and avoid aggressive actions, even when things move slower than you would like or when you feel you are being treated unfairly in some way. Best results come from being patient, tactful and willing to cooperate with others.

February 1st, 10th, 19th, 28th
Guide Numbers: 9, 2, 3

Friendships are highlighted: you may want to attend a number of social events. Try not to spread yourself too thin and be considerate of those close to you. If someone's waiting for you at home, think twice before stopping off for a drink after work.

February 2nd, 11th, 20th, 29th
Guide Numbers: 9, 2, 4

You'll have to deal with practical matters, such as dirty dishes that have been piling up, a car that needs fixing or a child's runny nose. Try to take these things in stride or feelings of frustration and depression could result.

February 3rd, 12th, 21st
Guide Numbers: 9, 2, 5

You are likely to get bored if faced with the same old dull routine. Do something different for a change. Unpleasant news may come your way, or you may have trouble controlling your temper when someone gets on your nerves.

February 4th, 13th, 22nd
Guide Numbers: 9, 2, 6

Family matters are highlighted; you may be concerned about someone's health. You could find yourself working for a cause—baking a cake, stuffing envelopes, even participating in a Walkathon for the March of Dimes.

February 5th, 14th, 23rd
Guide Numbers: 9, 2, 7

Detail work goes well; it's a good time to accumulate facts or do research of any kind. Your intuition is high and you would do well to listen to that inner voice. Your first impression is apt to be right.

February 6th, 15th, 24th
Guide Numbers: 9, 2, 8

The 9 Year: Clean Up

Don't let your feelings interfere with good judgment. You have much to gain by paying attention to sound advice and by working with others to get things done.

February 7th, 16th, 25th
Guide Numbers: 9, 2, 9

An old relationship may come to an end—let go of it as graciously as you can. Emotions need to be kept in check lest a temperamental outburst cause an embarrassing scene. Use this day to tie up loose ends.

February 8th, 17th, 26th
Guide Numbers: 9, 2, 1

New plans may be taking form in your mind, but they could be accompanied by doubts and fears. A friend who is a source of inspiration and solace may help you see things in a different light.

February 9th, 18th, 27th
Guide Numbers: 9, 2, 2

Emotional sensitivity could lead to problems. Try to keep everything in perspective and don't let petty annoyances get you down. Success comes from working in association with others and a willingness to share.

MARCH
Guide Numbers: 9, 3

Friends and social activities are highlighted this month: you may hear from someone you've been out of touch with for a while. Creative endeavors and self-expression are favored now, and you are likely to feel a surge of optimism as the result of a new idea or inspiration. Spend some money on pampering yourself for a change.

March 1st, 10th, 19th, 28th
Guide Numbers: 9, 3, 4

Practical affairs are highlighted, but mundane chores could get you down unless you take some time out to relax or do something you enjoy. There could be some obstacle or disappointment where a friendship is concerned.

Your Daily Numerology

March 2nd, 11th, 20th, 29th
Guide Numbers: 9, 3, 5

This is a people-oriented day, and you can promote yourself and your ideas easily. Accept any social invitations that come your way—you may meet someone interesting. Take care not to eat or drink too much.

March 3rd, 12th, 21st, 30th
Guide Numbers: 9, 3, 6

Your tolerance of others may be tested when someone's behavior leaves a lot to be desired. On the other hand, you may have a pleasant experience, perhaps involving a child. Be willing to adjust to circumstances that are beyond your control.

March 4th, 13th, 22nd, 31st
Guide Numbers: 9, 3, 7

You may be conscious of the deeper meanings of things and are unlikely to be amused by shallow conversation or silly behavior. This is a good time to write down your thoughts or discuss your interests with a friend.

March 5th, 14th, 23rd
Guide Numbers: 9, 3, 8

You may be feeling nostalgic; sentimentality could make you a soft touch. Take care not to let emotions interfere with facts when a decision has to be made. If necessary, ask someone whose opinion you respect for advice. This is a day to try to remain under control.

March 6th, 15th, 24th
Guide Numbers: 9, 3, 9

Social activities are highlighted: you may hear from an old friend you've lost touch with for a while. Your temper could be shorter than usual, so make sure you count to ten before telling someone off.

March 7th, 16th, 25th
Guide Numbers: 9, 3, 1

Energy is high; it's important that you find some outlet for expressing yourself in a creative way. Join a club or take a class. Besides the other benefits, you never know who you may meet.

The 9 Year: Clean Up

March 8th, 17th, 26th
Guide Numbers: 9, 3, 2
   Pay attention to details and try to be a good listener even when you'd like to inerrupt. You may meet someone new through a friend. Dealings with women are likely to be beneficial.

March 9th, 18th, 27th
Guide Numbers: 9, 3, 3
   Friends and social activities are highlighted; you may find yourself the center of attention. Take care not to get carried away and talk too much or exaggerate. A new idea or romantic interest could be uplifting.

APRIL
Guide Numbers: 9, 4
   Practical matters need your attention this month; you could experience a feeling of discouragement when something fails to turn out the way you hoped. You may find yourself considering a move or a different course of action. Try not to let your emotions rule your head.

April 1st, 10th, 19th, 28th
Guide Numbers: 9, 4, 5
   Don't count on everything working out as planned. Cancellations, postponements and changes should be taken in stride. Try to find a positive outlet for releasing your anger, such as engaging in an active sport or physical activity.

April 2nd, 11th, 20th, 29th
Guide Numbers: 9, 4, 6
   There may be many demands made on your time and domestic matters that require your attention. Should mediating conflicts be your lot, take care not to force your ideas on others. Maintain a realistic attitude and a light heart.

April 3rd, 12th, 21st, 30th
Guide Numbers: 9, 4, 7
   You may be feeling irritable or misunderstood and could benefit from some time alone. Being rushed is likely to be a

source of frustration; you may prefer staying home and reading a book or watching television rather than being dragged somewhere you don't really want to go.

April 4th, 13th, 22nd
Guide Numbers: 9, 4, 8

This is a good day to organize your personal affairs and take care of whatever business you've allowed to pile up. A past mistake may need to be accounted for and rectified in some way. Use common sense in dealing with matters of the heart as well as with practical concerns.

April 5th, 14th, 23rd
Guide Numbers: 9, 4, 9

You may be feeling some apprehension about the outcome of a relationship that's on the rocks. Try getting to the root of the problem logically rather than emotionally if you want to work out a solution. It's important to have realistic expectations of yourself and others.

April 6th, 15th, 24th
Guide Numbers: 9, 4, 1

You may feel like taking the initiative on some project, but there could be an obstacle in your path. Meet opposition with originality and resourcefulness. Maintain a sense of humor.

April 7th, 16th, 25th
Guide Numbers: 9, 4, 2

This is a good day for handicrafts of any kind, and detail work, home projects or family outings could all prove enjoyable. Loved ones can become a source of pleasure.

April 8th, 17th, 26th
Guide Numbers: 9, 4, 3

You could have a bright idea about how to spend your leisure time in a more satisfying way. Communications are highlighted; you may be called upon to enlighten someone who is in the dark.

April 9th, 18th, 27th
Guide Numbers: 9, 4, 4

The 9 Year: Clean Up

You will be forced to face reality. Although you may be discouraged over existing conditions or confused over some problem, don't let your mood blind you to common sense.

MAY
Guide Numbers: 9, 5

New people, new expectations and new points of view are highlighted this month. It's okay to eliminate something boring or confining, but take care not to act recklessly or lose your temper. A change in plans may be upsetting, but it forces you to move in a new and better direction.

May 1st, 10th, 19th, 28th
Guide Numbers: 9, 5, 6

You may find yourself involved in some domestic project—preparing a big family dinner, laying a carpet or going camping with the kids. Do what you can to avoid arguments. Plans could be upset by someone's refusal to compromise.

May 2nd, 11th, 20th, 29th
Guide Numbers: 9, 5, 7

You may find yourself doing some wishful thinking and wondering why your life can't be easier. If you persist in dwelling on negative thoughts, a feeling of melancholy or depression could prevail. Try to see things in a positive light and remember that tomorrow can bring new opportunities.

May 3rd, 12th, 21st, 30th
Guide Numbers: 9, 5, 8

You may feel like pursuing some leisure-time activity, but find yourself faced with more practical tasks. Try not to hurry your work or careless mistakes could make it necessary for you to do it over.

May 4th, 13th, 22nd, 31st
Guide Numbers: 9, 5, 9

This is a good day to spread your knowledge or share a special talent. Unexpected news about a loss or the end of a relationship could put you in an emotional mood. Anticipate new experiences and be tolerant of the weaknesses of others.

May 5th, 14th, 23rd
Guide Numbers: 9, 5, 1

Today's experiences could include anything from a new hairstyle to a promotion—but whatever it is will not be the status quo. Use your wits to turn a disadvantage into an advantage and be willing to let go of someone or something that is no longer important in your life.

May 6th, 15th, 24th
Guide Numbers: 9, 5, 2

You may have a hard time making decisions and wish someone else could do it for you. Unexpected delays or changes in plans may be upsetting, but they are likely to force you in a new and better direction.

May 7th, 16th, 25th
Guide Numbers: 9, 5, 3

You will find yourself in the limelight, whether speaking in front of a group or turning heads at a party. Take special care not to forget anything important in your rush to get somewhere.

May 8th, 17th, 26th
Guide Numbers: 9, 5, 4

This is a day to make a concentrated effort to get rid of any obstacles in your path. You are influenced by your environment; neat surroundings are important to clear thinking.

May 9th, 18th, 27th
Guide Numbers: 9, 5, 5

Impulsive actions or a cutting remark could cause hurt feelings and disrupted plans. Try to keep your temper in check, even when others annoy you. It'll be to your advantage to be adaptable and keep an open mind.

JUNE
Guide Numbers: 9, 6

The 9 Year: Clean Up

Home, family and community affairs are highlighted this month. You are likely to be making many adjustments to the needs of others and may feel drained by the demands on your time. Situations change, and a former friend or associate may no longer be a part of your life. Having harmony in your daily affairs is necessary for your peace of mind.

June 1st, 10th, 19th, 28th
Guide Numbers: 9, 6, 7

You may be more inclined to do a job to perfection than to hurry through it in a haphazard fashion. Being rushed or kept waiting could prove frustrating. Try not to lose your temper when someone interferes with your plans.

June 2nd, 11th, 20th, 29th
Guide Numbers: 9, 6, 8

You could find yourself asked to organize something or give advice. Take charge, but don't dictate. Although you may have strong feelings about what is right or wrong, this is not a time to sit in judgment on others.

June 3rd, 12th, 21st, 30th
Guide Numbers: 9, 6, 9

You may experience a variety of emotions, from excitement to remorse, as a certain matter comes to a head. An important relationship could reach a turning point; you may attend or participate in some creative or political event.

June 4th, 13th, 22nd
Guide Numbers: 9, 6, 1

You may feel like doing some celebrating as you take on a new responsibility or are freed from an old one. However, try not to overlook the feelings of others. A class or workshop may be highlighted; you could become involved in some community affair.

June 5th, 14th, 23rd
Guide Numbers: 9, 6, 2

You may find yourself attending a family reunion which you may or may not enjoy. Although delays or people who fail to live up to your expectations could prove frustrating, try to put your own feelings aside and be willing to accommodate a loved one.

June 6th, 15th, 24th
Guide Numbers: 9, 6, 3

You are likely to be in a social mood and easily distracted from your chores. Take care not to forget anything important in your haste or excitement to get somewhere. An event involving friends or children could come up, or you may find yourself pursuing a creative project.

June 7th, 16th, 25th
Guide Numbers: 9, 6, 4

Duties and responsibilities are highlighted; this is not a time to procrastinate. You may become interested in doing volunteer work or helping your neighbors in some way. Being of service to others can be rewarding, especially if they show their appreciation.

June 8th, 17th, 26th
Guide Numbers: 9, 6, 5

Adjustments will be necessary due to an unexpected family matter. Try doing something a different way for better results; adopt a different course of action where a loved one is concerned.

June 9th, 18th, 27th
Guide Numbers: 9, 6, 6

Family or community responsibilities cannot be avoided; you may have to alter your plans to accommodate the needs of someone else. Entertaining others can be a source of pleasure as long as you avoid controversial topics.

JULY
Guide Numbers: 9, 7

Rest, relaxation and time alone are important to your wellbeing this month. You may not be feeling up to par and need to get away for awhile. This is a good time to take a trip or vacation in order to gain a new outlook on things. Although you may feel torn between your own needs and the needs of those close to you, have faith that undesirable situations will work themselves out.

The 9 Year: Clean Up

July 1st, 10th, 19th, 28th
Guide Numbers: 9, 7, 8

Although it's important to be organized so you can get a lot accomplished, don't let yourself become absorbed to such an extent that you ignore the needs of a loved one. A project you are involved in could be a stepping-stone to some future opportunity.

July 2nd, 11th, 20th, 29th
Guide Numbers: 9, 7, 9

You may feel as though you are in a period of transition and be anxious to finish some project or see a situation to its end. Don't try to hold on to anything, let it all go. Travel over or near water may be highlighted.

July 3rd, 12th, 21st, 30th
Guide Numbers: 9, 7, 1

Mental pursuits are highlighted: you may find yourself doing anything from becoming lost in a good book to thinking up a new approach to a stubborn problem. You are apt to spend a good part of your day alone or working on some project behind the scenes.

July 4th, 13th, 22nd, 31st
Guide Numbers: 9, 7, 2

You may be feeling sad about some area of your life that seems to be in the process of change. A broken promise may haunt you, but try not to overreact or dwell on the past. Doing something spiritually uplifting can keep you from feeling lonely or depressed.

July 5th, 14th, 23rd
Guide Numbers: 9, 7, 3

Emotions could be your worst enemy unless you find some creative outlet through which to express them. Writing is especially favored: you are likely to experience a sense of release through jotting down your thoughts.

July 6th, 15th, 24th
Guide Numbers: 9, 7, 4

This is a good day to work on some quiet project, such as cleaning out a closet, taking care of your plants or putting your vacation photographs into a scrapbook. The idiosyncrasies of others are likely to annoy you more than usual now, especially if they disrupt your schedule.

July 7th, 16th, 25th
Guide Numbers: 9, 7, 5

You are likely to be in for a surprise—pleasant or unpleasant. A feeling of restlessness or discontent may lead you to embark on a short trip or adventure, and there could be some change in your living conditions.

July 8th, 17th, 26th
Guide Numbers: 9, 7, 6

You could find certain family members annoying; there may be some situation that requires you to make an adjustment. A minor mechanical problem, such as trouble with your car or an elevator, could cause a delay.

July 9th, 18th, 27th
Guide Numbers: 9, 7, 7

You may be feeling a bit unsure of yourself or about the future. Try to separate facts from fantasies so you can see things in their proper perspective. Rest is important to your well-being; this is a good time to get off by yourself for a while.

AUGUST
Guide Numbers: 9, 8

Good judgment and efficiency are the keynotes to success this month. A legal matter may require your attention, or you could find yourself doing some negotiating to wrap up a project. Make sure you use good common sense. Business matters may have emotional overtones, so take care not to confuse your head with your heart. Those close to you require help and advice, but you may be too busy to notice. Recognition for past efforts is very likely.

August 1st, 10th, 19th, 28th
Guide Numbers: 9, 8, 9

The 9 Year: Clean Up

You may have to tend to some unfinished business. It's better to get it over with than to let it drag on. Your tolerance and compassion may be tested; you could have a hard time keeping your emotions under control. Avoid being dramatic in public places unless you're on stage.

August 2nd, 11th, 20th, 29th
Guide Numbers: 9, 8, 1
This is a day to be assertive and take care of your own needs. Don't expect anyone else to make your decisions for you. Although you may feel you are alone in your views, it is important to stick by what you think is right.

August 3rd, 12th, 21st, 30th
Guide Numbers: 9, 8, 2
Try not to expect too much or you are likely to be disappointed. Many details need to be taken care of; it's important to remain patient and cooperative. Let others help you.

August 4th, 13th, 22nd, 31st
Guide Numbers: 9, 8, 3
This is likely to be a busy time; you may find yourself wondering where the day has gone. Take care not to schedule more activities or appointments than you can handle. A social event may prove profitable for business as well as pleasure.

August 5th, 14th, 23rd
Guide Numbers: 9, 8, 4
This is a day to face facts and be realistic. You may find yourself doing something you don't especially enjoy, or there could be a problem that's worrying you. Try not to let an unexpected obstacle or expense get you down.

August 6th, 15th, 24th
Guide Numbers: 9, 8, 5
The day may bring about a change in your home situation or career. You could have trouble keeping your emotions under control, whether it be joy, sorrow or anger that you feel. You may be embarking on a trip—possibly in connection with a family or business matter.

Your Daily Numerology

August 7th, 16th, 25th
Guide Numbers: 9, 8, 6

Responsibilities are highlighted; it may be difficult for you to find much time for yourself. A loved one could need your understanding or advice, and you may be asked to donate your services or money to a club or community program.

August 8th, 17th, 26th
Guide Numbers: 9, 8, 7

Slow down and read the fine print on any papers that need to be signed and make sure matters are to your advantage. If you have any doubts, get expert advice. Someone's big ego or personality quirk could prove especially annoying.

August 9th, 18th, 27th
Guide Numbers: 9, 8, 8

An opportunity to increase your financial status may present itself, but be wary of "get-rich-quick" schemes. It may be wise to get a second opinion. Don't postpone an important errand.

SEPTEMBER
Guide Numbers: 9, 9

Feelings of loss or disappointment are a possibility this month; you may have to part with a certain person or situation. Although you could be quite emotional and reminisce, this is not a time to hold on to the past. Concentrate on future plans. They should become more clear and certain as the month draws to an end. Try to have a "live-and-let-live" attitude.

September 1st, 10th, 19th, 28th
Guide Numbers: 9, 9, 1

A legal or health matter may be on your mind: you could find yourself consulting a lawyer or doctor. This is a time to expand your horizons and open yourself to new ideas and philosophies. You may have to let go of something old so you can become involved in something new.

September 2nd, 11th, 20th, 29th
Guide Numbers: 9, 9, 2

The 9 Year: Clean Up

Your patience may be tested by delays, red tape or petty arguments. Try to take annoyances in stride and to see things from a broader perspective. Loose ends need to be tied up before new ways of thinking can be put into action.

September 3rd, 12th, 21st, 30th
Guide Numbers: 9, 9, 3
Social activities and creative efforts are highlighted. You should have no trouble getting your ideas across, but let others have their say too. A festive occasion may be on your mind and make working long hours on anything tedious more difficult to take.

September 4th, 13th, 22nd
Guide Numbers: 9, 9, 4
You may have to face some unpleasant fact or become discouraged when your efforts don't seem to be getting you as far or as fast as you'd like. However, persistence will pay off.

September 5th, 14th, 23rd
Guide Numbers: 9, 9, 5
Be adaptable to change and willing to let go of the past. New people who come into your life could be fun to be with, but when you need them again they may not be around. An unexpected gift or some good fortune may be the highlight of your day.

September 6th, 15th, 24th
Guide Numbers: 9, 9, 6
Try not to force your ideas on others or be unrealistic in your expectations. Enjoy your companions for what they are and do something nice for someone without expecting anything in return. Those who are single could find romance. Those with partners may embark on a family project or trip.

September 7th, 16th, 25th
Guide Numbers: 9, 9, 7
Although you may be feeling lonely or nostalgic, be assured that change will be forthcoming. Try not to jump to hasty conclusions. Meditation or a good massage could help you relax.

September 8th, 17th, 26th
Guide Numbers: 9, 9, 8

This is a good day to channel your energy into some worthwhile cause or to donate some money to your favorite charity. You may have an urge to share your resources, and a need to be useful, coupled with an interest in public affairs, could lead you to become involved with a political group.

September 9th, 18th, 27th
Guide Numbers: 9, 9, 9

This is likely to be an emotional day; you could be more temperamental than usual. Try to avoid any impulsive outbursts of temper or fits of jealousy or possessiveness. Expand your horizons and get involved with something that can improve your mind.

OCTOBER
Guide Numbers: 9, 1

New interests and activities are highlighted this month; if you're unattached a new romantic interest could boost your spirits. Unexpected circumstances force you to take a stand, and what you give out can be expected to be returned to you later. Although you are likely to be feeling more independent, cooperation is still important, especially with someone who shares a common interest and who can be of help to you.

October 1st, 10th, 19th, 28th
Guide Numbers: 9, 1, 2

Little things may interfere with your plans; you could feel torn between your own desires and those of your loved ones. Try to *listen* to what others have to say. Not only will they appreciate your support, but you can also benefit from theirs.

October 2nd, 11th, 20th, 29th
Guide Numbers: 9, 1, 3

Friends and children are highlighted, as are your creative talents. A new idea or inspiration is likely to put you in a more energetic and optimistic frame of mind. Take care, however, not to spread yourself too thin.

The 9 Year: Clean Up

October 3rd, 12th, 21st, 30th
Guide Numbers: 9, 1, 4

You will need to exercise self-discipline if you are to complete all your chores. However, try not to be rigid or stubborn about letting others help you. An emotional conflict or a feeling of being overwhelmed may lead to a change of outlook where your goals are concerned.

October 4th, 13th, 22nd, 31st
Guide Numbers: 9, 1, 5

Today is likely to bring an unexpected twist or turn. Something could happen that leads to a change in your lifestyle, or you may find yourself exploring a new activity or opportunity. Take care lest distractions make you accident prone.

October 5th, 14th, 23rd
Guide Numbers: 9, 1, 6

Don't turn down the opportunity to work or socialize with someone interesting. Any added responsibility will be well worth the effort it entails, as you are likely to learn something from the experience. Group activities are highlighted: you could find yourself playing the role of host.

October 6th, 15th, 24th
Guide Numbers: 9, 1, 7

You are unlikely to have the time or energy to deal with anything you consider petty; small children could get on your nerves. Somethig you read in a magazine or newspaper may especially interest you.

October 7th, 16th, 25th
Guide Numbers: 9, 1, 8

Buying or selling something may be an issue; you should make sure the price is fair. You could lose out if you're too greedy. You are more likely to feel in control of things if you are organized and your affairs are in order.

October 8th, 17th, 26th
Guide Numbers: 9, 1, 9

Magnetism is high; you may be in the limelight at some time. Although it may take courage to break away from old patterns and try something new, you will be able to summon up the necessary willpower.

October 9th, 18th, 27th
Guide Numbers: 9, 1, 1

This is the time to direct your efforts towards future goals. Your energy is high and creative endeavors should meet with success. Try not to be temperamental or lash out at someone who gives you well-intentioned advice.

NOVEMBER
Guide Numbers: 9, 2

Sharing with others is the keynote to success and happiness this month. It's no time to remain aloof or to assert your will. Others need you and you need them. It is important to have patience when faced with obstacles and delays. This is a good time for gathering information you may need later.

November 1st, 10th, 19th, 28th
Guide Numbers: 9, 2, 3

This is a good day to be creative and to express your thoughts, but it is also important to listen to what others have to say. Be conscientious about keeping commitments. Your social life is highlighted: there is likely to be a lot of interaction going on.

November 2nd, 11th, 20th, 29th
Guide Numbers: 9, 2, 4

You may feel that someone is being too hard on you or that a situation is more than you can handle. It's impossible to please everyone, so don't even try. Attempting to be all things to all people could backfire.

November 3rd, 12th, 21st, 30th
Guide Numbers: 9, 2, 5

This is a time to be adaptable, as attempts to fight change will only lead to emotional strain. Take care of details as they come up. Some news may cause you to alter your plans, or you may have an unexpected visitor or invitation.

The 9 Year: Clean Up

November 4th, 13th, 22nd
Guide Numbers: 9, 2, 6
   You could be involved in a community or political cause, or you may find yourself defending your ideas on some family matter. Group activities are highlighted; you are unlikely to spend this day alone.

November 5th, 14th, 23rd
Guide Numbers: 9, 2, 7
   Trust your intuition—your psychic ability is high. This is a good time to gather, analyze and absorb information or do detail work of any kind. Think twice before engaging in anything shady, especially where a relationship is concerned.

November 6th, 15th, 24th
Guide Numbers: 9, 2, 8
   You may have a tendency to confuse your head and your heart. Take care not to be so concerned about the image you want to project that you let someone talk you into spending more money than you can afford.

November 7th, 16th, 25th
Guide Numbers: 9, 2, 9
   You could be more emotional than usual; feelings of nostalgia may put you in a sentimental mood. However, try not to be overly dramatic at an inappropriate time. Use your imagination and be creative as you go about your chores.

November 8th, 17th, 26th
Guide Numbers: 9, 2, 1
   Be sure you know what you're getting into before committing yourself to anything and don't be afraid to ask others for advice. Someone may come into your life who will remain important for a long time to come.

November 9th, 18th, 27th
Guide Numbers: 9, 2, 2
   This is a good day to get little things done or take care of detail work of any kind. Sharing with others is important; you are likely to feel lonely or depressed if there's no one around.

Your Daily Numerology

DECEMBER
Guide Numbers: 9, 3

Creative self-expression in any form is your keynote to success this month: you will have the opportunity to advance yourself through your talents. Inspiration flows, friends are helpful and it's a good time for enjoying life. However, you must take care not to be overly extravagant or to scatter your energies in too many directions. You may receive recognition for something you did well.

December 1st, 10th, 19th, 28th
Guide Numbers: 9, 3, 4

A friend or loved one may be the source of some emotional turmoil, but take care not to let your problems interfere with your daily routine. Practical matters must be dealt with, and you should be willing to face facts realistically.

December 2nd, 11th, 20th, 29th
Guide Numbers: 9, 3, 5

Unexpected things are likely to happen and could turn out to your advantage if you are on the alert. Be adaptable to changes in plans and try not to lose your temper when someone cancels out at the last moment.

December 3rd, 12th, 21st, 30th
Guide Numbers: 9, 3, 6

You will have to make some sort of adjustment in connection with a family or community matter. Strive for harmony in your surroundings, even though you may feel you would like more time for yourself.

December 4th, 13th, 22nd, 31st
Guide Numbers: 9, 3, 7

You may have to deal with a frustrating situation—perhaps being at a social gathering you don't particularly enjoy or being upset over someone's behavior. Try not to be too critical of yourself or others and make the best of an uncomfortable time.

The 9 Year: Clean Up

December 5th, 14th, 23rd
Guide Numbers: 9, 3, 8

Business and pleasure can be combined, but don't let your emotions get in the way of making practical decisions. This is a time to be in control of your affairs and use good judgment. You may be taking a trip in the line of duty.

December 6th, 15th, 24th
Guide Numbers: 9, 3, 9

You may be feeling more restless than usual. Take care not to let your imagination run wild, lest an uncontrolled outburst of temper cost you a valued friendship. News from a distance may be highlighted, or you could bump into someone you haven't seen in a while.

December 7th, 16th, 25th
Guide Numbers: 9, 3, 1

Although you may go to great lengths to get your point across, don't take it personally if your adience appears a bit distracted or doesn't seem to share your enthusiasm. The reason may not be what you think.

December 8th, 17th, 26th
Guide Numbers: 9, 3, 2

This is a day for sharing with others. Make sure you show your appreciation for considerations and thoughtful gestures. Although there could be some unexpected aggravation, count your blessings and try to put things in their proper perspective.

December 9th, 18th, 27th
Guide Numbers: 9, 3, 3

Energy is high and you are likely to be feeling in an optimistic mood. Take care not to spread yourself too thin. You may have a tendency to be extravagant or loquacious.

ABOUT THE AUTHORS

Sandra Kovacs Stein is the author of *Instant Numerology* (1979). Carol Ann Schuler is co-author of *The Vibes Book* (1979). Together they co-authored *Love Numbers* (1980). Both live and work in New York City.